If You Could See Me Now

Sherry Anthony

WESTBOW
PRESS
A DIVISION OF THOMAS NELSON
& ZONDERVAN

Copyright © 2014 Sherry Anthony.

All rights reserved. No part of this book may be used or reproduced by any means, graphic, electronic, or mechanical, including photocopying, recording, taping or by any information storage retrieval system without the written permission of the publisher except in the case of brief quotations embodied in critical articles and reviews.

WestBow Press books may be ordered through booksellers or by contacting:

WestBow Press
A Division of Thomas Nelson & Zondervan
1663 Liberty Drive
Bloomington, IN 47403
www.westbowpress.com
1 (866) 928-1240

Because of the dynamic nature of the Internet, any web addresses or links contained in this book may have changed since publication and may no longer be valid. The views expressed in this work are solely those of the author and do not necessarily reflect the views of the publisher, and the publisher hereby disclaims any responsibility for them.

Copyright 2014Cover Photo Credit Goes To Sherry Anthony and cannot be used without Authors Permission.

ISBN: 978-1-4908-5105-1 (sc)
ISBN: 978-1-4908-5106-8 (hc)
ISBN: 978-1-4908-5104-4 (e)

Library of Congress Control Number: 2014916085

Printed in the United States of America.

WestBow Press rev. date: 12/15/2014

Contents

Preface vii
A Special Thanks ix
Chapter 1 1
Chapter 2 9
Chapter 3 15
Chapter 4 21
Chapter 5 29
Chapter 6 37
Chapter 7 43
Chapter 8 51
Chapter 9 57
Chapter 10 63
Chapter 11 71
Chapter 12 79
Chapter 13 85
Chapter 14 95

Preface

As a young girl growing up, I didn't have a proper upbringing in a loving and caring home. My mother spent most of her time hanging out in bars and left me when I was six years old. My father was a truck driver, and his time was spent on the road. I had six siblings, and we were by ourselves most of the time. All of us, except my older brother who went to live with my grandmother, were placed in the children's home. From there we were put into different foster homes throughout the Ohio Valley, and we had no contact with one another. I felt abandoned. The yearning for my siblings and my parents weighed heavily on my heart. I longed for the family that was taken from me.

At age twelve, I gave my life to Christ, and through his love, I found some kind of peace in my life. But it wasn't until I became pregnant with my son, Preston, that my life felt whole. Preston was my world, and I wanted his life to be different from the life I had growing up. I could not leave him under any circumstances. I wanted to comfort him and give him the unconditional love that I never experienced as a child. It was important for me to spend time with him and to prove to him that I could be the responsible, caring, and loving mother that every child needs.

This autobiography is a tribute to Preston Anthony, to commemorate his life. This memoir will keep his bright spirit alive and allow his dream of becoming a veterinarian technician to thrive. His love for animals was apparent throughout his life. Preston was a joy, and he captivated my heart and soul. He brought love and peace to the many lives he touched. His life was not always easy, and he faced many trials. The village that it took to guide his life would turn out to be monumental in turning his life around. We came to rely on God's grace and his strength to pull us through all our struggles.

Preston was a bright boy who had the world at his fingertips, but he struggled with not having his father in his life and not knowing how to communicate or deal with the problems he had to face in our world. He kept everything inside of him, and this made it hard for those who tried to reach out to him. The school of hard knocks taught him many lessons before God called him home. Through Preston's life, we can reflect on the lessons that God has sent us down on earth to learn. Preston's life as we knew it has ended, but his memory and dream can live on through the lives he wished to touch. It is through this commemoration that his history and memory can make a difference in your life.

A Special Thanks

I would like to Thank God for he is the one who is most deserving of all for bringing the most precious Gift any one could ever have into my life. The Gift of life, that I called Preston. Preston was my world and touched my soul. He truly was the part of my heart that made it whole. Our life together was filled with Love, Joy, Laughter and Tears, but with God in our lives, we could always count on him to be there for us throughout the years.

A thank you goes out to all who have given me the drive to complete my book and who has given me the inspiration that I needed. Westbow Press, publishing company, this book would not be without you. Thank you! KTIS, Radio Station. For the uplifting music and the encouraging messages you give. Francesca Battistelli, (Write Your Story) Deana Martin (Memories are made of this), Mark Eddy, Cyndi Lewinski for the inspiration that you gave. George Fisher. For the encouraging posts that you shared. Jack Canfield. (Chicken soup for the soul) Shemar Moore. (The tenacity and drive you have for MS) Joe and Victoria Osteen, (Encouraging words for the love of God) Barbara Gains (The Messenger of God) and all of my social Media friends and family for giving me the drive in completing this labor of love. I love you all and could not have done this without you.

A Special Thanks also goes out to the ones who were a part of my son's life and to all who have given their time in making a difference in our lives. Ricky, for the love you and Preston had for one another, and The legacy he left behind.(Preston Jr.) He loved you and you made him happy. Thank You, I love you both. Preston is on the other side hugging and smiling down on you for doing such a wonderful job. Zack, Preston always looked forward to coming to your home and hanging out with you and your friendship meant the world to him. He is still with you. Jeff, you two were the best of friends, and were selected for the school of the gifted. He enjoyed coming over to your house. You will always be remembered. Anthony, you two were the smartest in your class. He loved you and will always be with you. Anthony and Christina, you two were special to my son and he always looked forward to playing with you. He thought the world of you and I am sure he is looking down on you both. Mike, you two were like brothers and you two had a special bond that no one could break. I am sure he is with you always. Daniel, you two were close and together till the end and I am sure he is with you. Joshua, Preston always did have a heart of gold in helping everyone that he could. He thought the world of you and is with you always. Marcus, you were the inspiration and the true light that was in my son's life. He looked up to you and respected you with and undying love like no other. Lil Rich, Preston thought the world of you and I am sure he is with you, ATL, for your friendship that you had with my son and I am sure he is with you. Joey, you and Preston were cousins and spent a lot of time together growing up. You two were crazy and never ceased to amaze me with the things you did. He loved you and so do I. Chuck, My brother, Vanessa, Kirstin, and Savanna, for taking my son in when he needed help. He loved you all. Thank you for extending your love to him. I know he is looking down on you all. Mr. Williams who took the time out of his life to teach my son to be what we all knew he could be. I am sure Preston is Grateful to you for the things you taught him. I extend a thank you for the impact you had on his life. Grant, you were a true friend to Preston and I am sure he is looking over you. Dave, Preston's Grandfather for his undying love and support you gave to him throughout his life. He loved you and looked up to you for guidance. Preston and I would like to thank you for giving up your plot so that he could be buried next to his Grandma Janice. He loved both of you very much, and so do I. Bridget, for your friendship and for being in our lives in the beginning of Preston's life. Thanks for the love and caring that you gave. I am sure he is looking down from heaven and smiling upon you. On Preston's behalf, I want to say thank you to all who touched his life and were there for him. You all meant the world to him and I am sure he is with you all. I thank you all from the bottom of my heart for touching and being a part of our lives.

Aknowledge Kelly Dunn Art And Photographer.

If You Could See Me Now…

*If you could see me now, you wouldn't shed a tear.
Though you may not understand why I'm no longer here.
Remember my spirit, that's the real me.
I'm still very much alive, oh, if you could only see!
I've beheld our father's face. I've touched my savior's hand.
The angels all rejoiced as I entered the promised land.
Beyond the gates of pearl, I walk on golden streets.
I've touched the walls of jasper, dipped my foot in the crystal sea.
The beauty is beyond words, nothing can compare.
I've even seen your mansion; someday I will meet you there.
Allow Jesus to be your guide, his word will show you the way.
So, please, don't cry! We will meet again someday!*

© *Patsy Stambaugh Deskins*

Chapter 1

On September 25, 1984, I gave birth to an eight-pound baby boy measuring twenty-one and a half inches. I named him Preston. I was exhausted but eager to be the kind of mother I wanted to be. I prepared everything in advance for this moment that had finally arrived. Preston was as perfect as I imagined he would be. He had olive skin that was as smooth as silk. He was the missing part of my heart that made it whole.

When the doctor placed Preston on my stomach after birth, my precious boy seemed to weigh a ton. I was as proud as I could be. I cried like a little baby from the excitement of having him. My heart pounded with joy as the nurse placed him in my trembling arms. As the tears streamed down my face, I counted all his fingers and toes as he wriggled against my chest. I took my finger and touched his cheek, and he smiled. When I could speak, I whispered, "Welcome, Preston." He was perfect in every way. I chose the name Preston from a baby book that I came across while looking for names close to God. Mark, Luke, and John were all too common as far as I was concerned. I was looking for something unique, something that would honor my son. The name Preston stood for the structure of the church, so I chose that for my son.

My pregnancy was easy. I did not have morning sickness, but I did want to eat healthy, balanced meals so that Preston could be as healthy as could be. I was up every morning early and excited about being a mother. Preston was my world even before he was born. To get ready for him, I learned many things about taking care of a baby and about becoming a mother. I lived in a one-story apartment and stocked a built-in corner cupboard with diapers, baby wipes, lotions, and other things that I would need for him. In my world, being a mother was going to be the best experience of my life.

I remember the day I brought him home. I did not have a crib for him because my apartment was too small for one, but I had bought a bassinet that he fit so beautifully in. He was precious, and I was honored to be given the opportunity to be his mother. What a true gift from God he was.

Preston was the most important thing to me. I was sure he was going to teach me things I never knew. The first time I brought him home from the hospital, all he did was sleep. *Well now*, I thought, *he is sleeping too much. I better call the hospital.* So that is what I did. I asked the attending nurse on duty that day about him sleeping as long as he was and if there was something wrong with my baby.

She asked me, "When was the last time you fed him?"

I said, "About six hours ago."

She said, "Wake him up every four hours and feed him."

Now I would have never thought of that. I had never had anyone wake me up to feed me, so I just thought babies were the same. I was learning the first thing about being a mother: not to starve the baby. I was so happy to find out nothing was wrong with my baby and that the problem was with me. I got off the phone and died laughing at myself. I had several bottles already prepared in the refrigerator, so I went and fed him immediately.

I must have called the nurse at the most opportune time, because in feeding him every four hours I was blessed with him sleeping all night until morning. I too needed my rest, and this feeding schedule worked out for the both of us. He would wake up every morning at seven and want to be fed. I do not think he enjoyed the burping process though. Every time I would take the bottle out of his mouth to burp him, he would let out this bloodcurdling scream. I knew I wasn't doing anything wrong and could not figure this out. Then it dawned on me that he was upset that I'd taken the bottle out of his mouth. This made me chuckle a bit, and I would just pat his little back and tell him I would give him more as soon as he burped. This did not seem to make him happy, and he just kept crying.

At three months, Preston was curious, an alert baby who picked up on things very quickly. I didn't realize it at the time, but Preston was becoming as brilliant as brilliant could be. He was eating table food at five months old and walking on his own before he was a year old. You had to show Preston something only once, and he would go with it after that.

I did not have a job at this time and was on government assistance until I could find employment, so his learning and education fell solely upon me. I spent a lot of time with Preston, read him many books, and bought educational things to help him learn. As the days passed and Preston became stronger, I learned he could do things on his own. I had never watched little ones at this age and didn't know what they could do. With Preston, at three months old he was rolling over and lifting his strong head up to see what he could see. I learned that Preston would not go to sleep unless I was up making some kind of noise for him to hear. He must have received some sort of comfort in knowing that someone was near.

Preston was curious about his world, and at six months, Preston and I moved up above a furniture store, off of Sunset Boulevard. The other apartment did not accommodate what we needed and had steam heaters. Preston was starting to walk, and I did not want him to get burned. The apartment above the furniture store was perfect. It was spacious, had gas heat, and provided Preston with a room of his own. Our time in that apartment was wonderful.

Preston was holding on to the coffee table one day and trying to take some steps on his own. I thought I'd see if he could really do it on his own, so I took both of his hands and guided him to the middle of the floor and let him go. I kept saying, "Here we go." He took off as if it was nothing. I thought it was wonderful to see him want to walk. He had this big smile on his face that just seemed to light the whole room. I praised him and clapped my hands. I could clearly see that he was ready for his first pair of walking shoes. I took him the next day to the store and bought him the best pair of Buster Brown shoes I could find. It was history after that. I found myself chasing after him everywhere. It was as though he had Energizer Batteries in those shoes. I was exhausted from chasing after him every day, but I would not change it at all, not for anything in the world.

I so loved those years watching him grow and learn everything in the privacy of our home in Steubenville, Ohio. I spent the days reading to Preston and teaching him the motor skills that he needed to learn. I bought him things that I thought would help further his education. This time was gratifying, and I loved every minute of those precious years that he and I shared together. I wanted to make an everlasting impression on his life. I took him to family functions at the church, to the park for picnics, and friends' homes to visit. Everywhere I took Preston everyone acknowledged that he was a happy and alert baby. I could not have been a prouder parent.

Preston was sounding out syllables at the age of one. It was very important for me as a mother to teach him things that I myself was deprived of as a child. This was our family time, and what an experience it was.

Preston and I went to the store one day, and I ran into one of my foster sisters that I had not seen in a while. I inquired about my foster mom and dad and found that they had moved. My foster sister did not have a telephone number to give to me, but she said that they all were going to have a family reunion and an elephant sale at GKL Park. She told me the date, and I told her I would see her there. The day finally arrived for us to attend, and it was so nice to see my foster mom and dad. My mom, Janice, and dad, Dave, absolutely fell in love with Preston that day. It was the first time since I actually lived with them that they had seen me. I don't think they knew that I'd been pregnant and had a baby.

My mom and dad were in a raft boat when I arrived. I walked up to greet them with Preston in my arms. My mom held out her arms to Preston, and he went straight to her. They sat in the boat visiting, and I just hung around and visited with family members that I had not seen in a while. It was nice for us to get together and catch up on what we were all doing in our lives. Little did I realize at the time, but this was going to be something special for Preston. To have grandparents that were actually a part of his life meant the world to me, as I did not have that growing up. I was glad that this chance had come into our lives; it would be very beneficial for both of us. That day my mom, dad, and I caught up on what was going on in our lives and arranged to keep in touch with one another.

Not long after that visit, my foster mom called and said she was coming over for a visit. Preston and she became acclimated once more, and he was clearly getting quite comfortable with her. My mom continued coming over to visit, and this was a pleasant experience for both of them. Every time she came she had lots of goodies for him—candy, cakes, and all the good things that grandmas give to their grandkids. Preston always looked forward to her visits. My mom was absolutely trying to win Preston's heart. Many of my biological relatives did not take an integral part in our lives, and these special moments with my foster mom meant the world to me.

It felt nice to think that Preston and I actually had someone that cared for us. I never felt as if I had that growing up. I was placed in seventeen different foster homes throughout my life and always felt empty and isolated and yearned for my family. Janice came into my life after the children's home terminated my case. I ran into a boy that I knew from the children's home, and he was living with Janice and Dave at the time. I told him that I did not have anywhere to live and was searching for a place to stay. He said he'd talk to Janice and Dave. I patiently waited outside to hear what they would say. Janice and Dave extended their home to me that day. I was seventeen years old at the time. Them taking it upon themselves to take me into their home without knowing anything about me and now to accept my son spoke volumes to my heart. I called her mom, and she and my dad gave unconditional love as no other people I have ever met. I saw the world in a new light and had hope for the family that I so longed for all those years.

Ida, Grandpa Dave, and Preston

Bridget and Preston

Chapter 2

Preston was growing quite fond of his newfound grandma. My mom started taking Preston on visits to her house for the weekends or whenever she could. Those visits were some of Preston's most memorable times. My mom had three other children that she had adopted—Chucky, Kimberly, and Ida. They all enjoyed and looked forward to Preston's visits.

My mom had a farmhouse that did not have the accommodations of a normal home. It was under construction, and they had no shower, running water, or bathroom inside. The first time I stayed overnight, I asked where the shower was. My brother Chuck handed me a pot and a jug of water and told me to fill it up and heat it on the stove. I looked at him as if he were crazy. I asked where I was supposed to take this pot of water after it was heated. He directed me to the porch and said, "There is your shower." I died laughing, and all I could think was *The Beverly Hillbillies*. I also wondered where they got the water in the first place. I thought that the jugs of water could be quite expensive since there were so many. I found out that they drove to collect water from a spring on a dirt road quite a distance from where they lived.

The outhouse was a sight to see. Whenever I visited, I hoped that I wouldn't have to use the bathroom late at night. That farmhouse truly gave me an appreciation for the city life. On the weekends that my mom could not take Preston, Joey, Preston's cousin, would visit. Preston and Joey were about the same age, and they would play and hang out together. One time Preston was at Joey's house without me. As the story goes, they were sitting at the table eating peanut-butter-and-jelly sandwiches. They were playing with their food, and somehow or another the food landed on the ceiling fan, which was on. My brother and his wife were not happy about that. That incident was the end of Preston's visits without me being present. *Now kids will be kids*, I told myself, but my brother did not see it like that. My brother did not physically discipline either of them, but he told them both that kind of behavior would not be tolerated. I thought not letting Preston come over without me being present was a little harsh, and could have been handled differently, but it was my brother's decision, and I respected his wishes.

Joey continued to visit at our house, and he and Preston really had a great time together. Now, sometimes one of them would get hurt. They would run about the house, and I had to tell them to quit running. Preston opened the front door one day and accidentally hit Joey's eye with the doorknob. Preston just stood there, not realizing what had happened. I knew he didn't really mean to hurt his cousin. I called Joey's mother and told her about what had happened, and we both concluded that Joey did not need any medical treatment, as his eye would heal on its own.

Joey and Preston spent a lot of time in Preston's bedroom. They were three years old at this time. They would go in there, and they would be so quiet at times. I'd check on them now and then to see what they were doing. I opened Preston's door one time to find Preston smothering Joey with a pillow. I told them, "This behavior is unacceptable, and someone could seriously get hurt." *Crazy*, I thought. I do not know what in the world Preston was thinking to do such a thing to his cousin. Preston and I discussed this, and as far as I was aware, this never happened again. I loved seeing the boys together and took them places so that they both could get the feel of nature. We would go fishing, to the park, and to the zoo. Joey appeared to enjoy the visits, and he and Preston became very close throughout these years. These were important years for both of them, and I got so much joy watching them grow up together.

Preston had two friends, Anthony and Christina, who lived next door to us. The three of them would play throughout the week, and this worked out well for when Joey could not be there. Our apartment above the furniture store was high up from the road and had a wall that led to the roof of the building. They all tried to climb onto that wall, and I had to watch closely when they were out there. My boyfriend at that time had made Preston a little table and a bench. I would take out sandwiches and cookies and juice for them so that they could have a snack when they stopped playing. Anthony and Christina grew quite fond of Preston and looked forward to seeing and playing with him as often as they could.

I loved birds and thought it would be fun to have one as a pet, so I purchased a yellow canary. I put its cage outside on a hook so that it could get some fresh air. I stepped inside the house for a quick minute to go to the bathroom, and when I came back outside, I found the birdcage had fallen off the hook. The birdcage door was open, and the canary was gone. I asked all three of the kids what happened. They each had a different story and blamed each other. I surmised that the cage must have fallen after they hit it with their heads while jumping around.

The bird had flown to a huge tree across the street from where we lived. I was so scared to see the bird in the tree that day. I was sure the other birds would kill it, because it had no survival skills. After all, I did feed it every day, so how in the world would it survive on its own? I did not know. I tried my best to call for it. The strange thing was that the bird had been getting very comfortable with me as its owner. Every day before this happened I would take the bird out of its cage, sit it on my finger, pet it, and talk to it. This was not going to happen anymore. I decided that I was never going to buy a bird again. That night when Preston said his bedtime prayers, he asked the Lord to return the bird to its cage, which we had left on the porch. I could tell from his prayers that he was sorrowful, but the damage had already been done. The bird never did return.

As the days went by, memories of the bird disappeared. My proprietor did not allow dogs or cats, but we did take in a stray tabby cat against his wishes. Preston always had a love for animals, so we attempted to keep her. One night while we were sleeping, the cat was wailing. I didn't know what to think. Later, I found out that she was in heat. *Well now*, I thought, *we cannot have that cat doing this; for sure, we will be thrown out of our house.* I put the cat outside, but she returned the next day. I could not resist the look on Preston's face when he saw the cat, so I let her back inside. Preston always had a way of warming my heart. We went to the store and purchased her a bed. She was part of the family now. Preston would pick her up and take her around the house everywhere he went. I had to save her on a few occasions because three-year-old Preston did not know how to handle a cat properly. He would pick her up around the neck, and she would meow. *Poor cat*, I thought.

About nine or ten weeks later, I discovered that she had gotten pregnant the night I let her outside when she was wailing. The night finally arrived to have her kittens. Two were gray and black, and the other three were solid black. The last one she tried to deliver did not make it. *What in the world are we going to do with all these kittens?* I thought. I didn't know, but I had to make sure they didn't make too much noise. I stuck them in the bathroom with their mother and tried to make the best of it until they were old enough that I could find them a home.

One day I was doing laundry and went to put away some towels in the bathroom closet. There were four shelves, and the towels went on the top shelf. I reached up to put the towels away, and when I stepped down, I realized I had stepped on a kitten's head. I never felt so bad in all my life. It was one of the gray-and-black kittens. I placed it into a shoe box, and Preston and I went to the vet that day. I explained to the vet what had happened and asked if he thought he would be able to save the kitten. Sadly, after he examined it, he said he couldn't do anything except give it a proper burial. I was heartbroken. Preston and I left, sobbing. "You killed our kitten," Preston said. I felt so horrible and helpless. Preston's face just tore me up inside. How could I explain to him that sometimes accidents happened? I could not ease his pain.

We continued taking care of the three kittens that were left, and soon they were big enough to eat on their own. It came time for us to find them a new home. I luckily found some nice people to take them, and what a relief it was. All we needed to do now was find someone to take the mother of the kittens.

I recall one day Preston and I were out shopping and came home to find our cat was not there. I searched frantically everywhere.

Preston looked under his bed, under the chair, anywhere that we thought she might try to hide. She was nowhere to be found. No matter how many times we called her name, she did not come. Preston and I thought that she might have gotten out when we opened the front door to go shopping.

Then about three days later, I got a phone call from my proprietor who was in the furniture store below us, and he asked if I had a cat. I did not know how to respond, because I knew we were not allowed to have a cat. "Why?" I asked. He said, "There is one in our furniture store, and I think that it came from your house." I went down to the store, and sure enough it was our cat. I told him our story about keeping the cat, but he said that we had to get rid of her. I told him I would do my best to find a new home for her.

Preston and I were never so heartbroken in all our lives. We had grown to love this cat, and the thought of her leaving us was unbearable. Preston kept begging me to keep her, saying, "We can hide her, Mommy." I explained that if we kept the cat, we would have to move. "Then where would we live?" I added. That day I made several calls to find the cat a home but had no luck. After a week went by, I knew what I had to do and called the pound, hoping they would find her a home. I arranged to drop the cat off that day. As Preston and I drove to the pound, I knew what we were thinking and how each of us felt. No words were needed on this ride.

Chapter 3

I told Preston I was sure the animal shelter would have better luck in finding our cat a home. Preston said he agreed, and I was never so pleased in all my life to hear him say that. Preston never forgot to say his prayers every night, and that night he asked the Lord to find our cat a good home.

Preston always said the cutest prayers before going to bed. He would pray for all the animals he could think of in this world, and all I could think was *Bless his little heart.* He would pray to God for his friends and family and for the unfortunate people who did not have anything. God was always number one in our home, and we were grateful for the opportunity to pray for the important things that weighed on our hearts. Preston's love for animals always came through in his prayers and the encounters he had with animals throughout his years growing up.

Preston slept every night with a stuffed seal he named Sammy. Sammy seemed to give him some comfort during this time. Not too long after we gave up the cat, the man I was seeing bought a male sheepdog. This sheepdog was all white, and the day my boyfriend brought him home, the dog's hair was all matted and dirty. Preston said, "Mommy, that dog is dirty and smells. I think we need to give it a bath." So we got the hose out and gave the dog a good wash. The dog was like new, and Preston named him Boomer.

Boomer was a good dog, but my boyfriend did not want Boomer inside his house for reasons that he did not explain to us. Instead, my boyfriend decided to tie the dog around the flagpole in his driveway. Boomer was fine throughout the day as long as someone was outside with him, but during the day, and at night when my boyfriend was not at home, Boomer would bark. This became a problem after a while, and the neighbors would fuss about him barking. This went on about three months, and then one day we came home after shopping to find that Boomer was not on his chain. Preston was so upset and cried. We all wondered where Boomer was. We rode all through the neighborhood hollering for him but could not see or hear him. We drove on State Route 7 down to the river, but no Boomer in sight. Preston was not a happy camper that day to say the least. I did not want to tell him what I suspected. The dog chain was not broken, and so I thought someone might have unhooked Boomer.

Boomer never did return, and Preston and I thought about him often. This was the eighth animal in our lives that something happened too. Preston never forgot to say prayers for Boomer. All we could hope for was that Boomer found a nice home. After losing him, we all decided that we were just not cut out for any more animals. Anthony and Christina had a cocker spaniel that they and Preston enjoyed having outside with them when they were playing, but Preston spent very little time with that dog.

As the days passed, time seemed to fly by, and Preston became very clingy with me. He was still three years old at this time. I was starting a new job and knew it was time for Preston to interact with children other than the ones he had around him on a regular basis. Besides, I told myself it would be good for him to be in a school-like setting. I called the Jefferson County day-care center that was next to the children's home where I used to live. I arranged for Preston and me to go in and see exactly what they had to offer. They had what we needed, so I enrolled him. I told them that I would be working for the state and would need their services until five o'clock Monday through Friday. The woman assured me that would be fine, as long as I was there before six. I filled out all the necessary paperwork, and a new journey was about to begin.

The first day was very scary for both of us. He cried so hard and thought that I was leaving him forever. I could not break away from those little tears and the pain in my heart, but I knew I had to leave. How do you explain to a three-year-old that Mommy has to go to work? He just would not understand. The day-care lady assured me he would be fine, and so I kissed him one more time and promised him Mommy would be back later to pick him up. I went to work and picked him up after. I asked the day-care woman how the day went. She told me he had been a little withdrawn but assured me that he would get better as the days went on. Preston was so excited to see me and ran straight to my arms and hugged me. It was a real joy to see him like this, but I wondered how the remaining days of this would pan out for him.

I had to be at work at seven in the morning. I got Preston up early and told him that he had to go to school again that day, and he started to cry. I reassured him and told him about all the fun things he was going to learn. He appeared fine with what I told him at first, but when we reached the door of the day-care center, it was pretty much like the day before. This went on about three weeks or so, and

I guess it finally dawned on him that I was coming for him every day after work, so he started to adjust to the changes.

Preston's first progress report from the day care said that he was an alert boy and his vocabulary was excellent for his age. I had consciously made a decision not to talk baby talk to him while growing up. So his vocabulary was always like an adult's. The daycare woman told me they had a set time that they would line up all the children to go to the bathroom, and the teacher would stand by the stalls just in case anyone needed assistance. Preston was directed to an empty stall to go to the bathroom, and the teacher opened the stall door to see if he needed her help. Preston said, "Excuse me, I need my privacy." The teacher and I both laughed so hard. She said Preston's vocabulary was like no other child's she had ever run across. I had always taught him to shut the door when he went into the bathroom. If he needed me, he would holler, and then I would come to assist him. Preston was truly one of a kind, and even then, he made everyone laugh. You never really knew what he was going to say next.

There was one little girl with long blonde hair and blue eyes that took an interest in my son. When all the children gathered in a circle to do an activity for the day, she would sway back and forth and bat her eyes at Preston. His first crush and he did not even know about it. This little girl invited Preston to her birthday party. When it came time to blow out the candles on her cake, Preston decided he would help her. He took a big breath and the flames went out, but in doing so, he spit on the cake, making the children exclaim, "Ew!" I know Preston did not mean to do it, but he apologized even though he didn't realize what he'd done. Preston was growing up and learning how to deal with others and becoming his own individual.

One of his teachers at the day-care center told me Preston was a leader and not a follower. He spent his playtime on the playground with dump trucks, and he would supervise and instruct the other children on what he thought needed done. When it rained and the children could not go outside, he would take the initiative to help the other children with picking up their toys, paintbrushes, and anything that he thought was helpful.

One time, the children were doing an activity that required glue. One of the little girls had glue on her hands and tried to remove it by picking it off. In doing so, she thought her skin was falling off. She hysterically cried, and Preston ran to her aid and consoled her by hugging her and telling her it would be all right. Preston was known at the day-care center as being one of the most helpful, caring, and loving children that they had run across. I was honored, proud, and happy to hear that Preston was doing well. These early years of his growth gave me an appreciation of what life had to offer us. The day-care center gave him the foundation of what he needed to succeed in these early years of his life.

Preston seemed happy at the day-care center. Every day after picking him up, we had conversations during dinner about his day. Preston told me he enjoyed all the staff that worked with him. He told me about the children he played with and what he learned. Preston's life was progressing nicely, and I was happy that he had the opportunity to lean all that was presented to him.

Boomer

Chapter 4

I continued working for the state for about seven weeks and was making very good money. I invested a lot of it in buying Preston interesting learning games, puzzles, and books to make him think. When I was three, my parents didn't buy me anything that helped in my learning; I had to learn things on my own. I wanted desperately to teach my son and give him every opportunity that I could to help him learn. I bought Preston blocks, and before he turned a year old, we had worked extensively on math skills by adding and subtracting them. I bought him books in which he had to follow numbers to create a connect-the-dot picture that he could then color. He had a real skill for staying within the lines. He loved to draw, and the connect-the-dot pictures gave him the opportunity to know a little bit about art.

I created flash cards with words, and this helped when we read books. Preston loved reading and was eager to help with a story. I loved every minute of these learning experiences. I had a real genius on my hands, I thought. The teachers and I were proud that Preston was learning things faster than the other children were. I guess everything that I was doing with him paid off, because his progress reports displayed all check marks.

The teachers felt some things needed to be addressed though. Preston was having some issues sharing with the other children.

I knew this was hard for Preston because he never had to share anything at home. So I started working on this issue more closely when his cousin Joey would come over, and at first, it was a real struggle. I had several conversations with Preston about how whoever picked up a toy had first dibs on it and that it wasn't fair to take something from someone that had it first. Usually if you had a conversation with Preston about what he was doing wrong, he would understand and do what was right. Preston was learning the rules of life and becoming sociably adaptable.

My job working for the state was seasonal and ended, so I again found myself looking for employment. I continued to let Preston go to the day-care center until the funds ran out. Finally, a local country club hired me, which meant, once again, I needed someone to watch Preston. I decided to place an ad for a babysitter in the paper. In a short time, the responses started pouring in.

After interviewing several possible candidates, I hired Tracey. I explained to her what I expected her to do, and she assured me that she was very capable. She seemed to be the perfect fit for the job, and Preston took a liking to her. I was very pleased about this. You know, it is funny how things just worked out for the benefit for all. Tracey and I became friends, and her family became our family. When I was not working and they had something planned, they would always include Preston and me.

Tracey; her mom, Shirley; and her dad, Fred; and I attended St. Paul's Episcopalian Church. Tracey, Shirley, and I were in the choir. On Wednesdays, we had choir practice and looked forward to singing. For Preston and I, the experience of going to this church became one of the most significant times in our lives.

I became friends with a man named Bill, who also was a part of our choir group at the time, and he took a liking to Preston. Bill would always have Preston sit by him during church functions and would talk to him. Bill was a real hoot and always had us in stitches from laughing. It was during this time that I had Preston baptized at the church. I asked Bill and Tracey's dad, Fred, to be Preston's godparents. Preston looked so handsome on his baptismal day, and I could not get over how big my little boy was growing up to be. I just wanted him to stay little forever. I dressed him up in a white suit and a nice shirt and a blue tie with gray dress shoes. He was a handsome little man. We had a baptizing celebration for Preston at Shirley and Fred's home, and it turned out well.

When I received the baptismal papers, one of the clergy members asked me if I was the daughter of Leonard and Delores Anthony. I was a little hesitant to answer because I didn't know where she was going with this. She told me that she was going through the records and found out that my parents had been married in this church. I could not believe it. Preston and I were actually attending the same church that my biological mom and dad were married in. *Wow, how magnificent*, I thought, *to know the parents that never raised me were actually married in this church.* I took this as a sign from God. He must have known what he was doing in guiding us to the right church and to the right people. I never in my life was so happy to be attending that church.

God truly has a way of working things out behind the scenes. I knew that he was looking out for Preston and me and had our best interests at heart. Preston and I both loved going to St. Paul's. Preston was in Christmas plays and other activities that the church held. We would go on field trips with the other church parents as chaperones. Our life was actually shaping up to be what God had planned for us all along. You never know what the Lord has in store for you, but Preston and I took a leap of faith and let God lead the way. I knew that in order to raise Preston, God and church was the way to go. I did not have the proper guidance at first growing up, so I wanted things to be different for my son. I loved our life and was trying as a mother to do what was right for Preston.

I was dating a gentleman named Bill, a different man from the Bill in my choir group. Bill used to teach shop at the local high school, was a substitute math teacher on call when needed, and worked at Wheeling Pittsburgh Steel Mill. Bill was a great influence on Preston. Bill taught Preston how to hammer nails into boards, and he and Preston built shelves for me to hang on my wall. Preston was learning how to be a carpenter. Preston could not run the band saw but would stand there and watch everything that Bill showed him how to do. Preston planted his first pine tree and learned to water it and watch it grow. Bill would tell Preston that one day that tree would be taller than he was. Preston would just listen to Bill talk, and his mind would soak everything up like a sponge. Preston and Bill were quite fond of one another. I could see that these two were a great team together.

I loved Bill for his willingness to be the role model that he was and for being the one who captured Preston's heart. I was hoping to marry Bill and give my son the father that he so desperately needed. This did not pan out, and it broke Preston's heart very much. Preston longed to have a permanent dad in his life, and he enjoyed the times that he and Bill spent together. They had a special relationship that no one could touch. Preston told me on several occasions that he loved Bill and would ask me if Bill could be his dad. I truly did not know what to say to him. I just said that some people were not meant to be married and were better off just staying friends. I told Preston we must be appreciative of the times that we did spend together. Bill and I separated shortly after Preston and I had this discussion. I knew in my heart that the relationship would not end up being any more than what it was.

Our lives continued as well as expected after the breakup, and Preston still kept in touch with Bill by phone. This appeared to work out well. Bill would stop by after shopping over at Federico's store across the street from where we lived. He would drop off goodies that he thought Preston would enjoy.

One time Bill stopped over to drop something off and left his car running and his driver-side door open. The car was parked down over the hill from our house. We both thought that Preston was right there beside us, but when we turned to see where Preston was, he was inside Bill's car standing in the driver's seat and going down the hill with both hands on the steering wheel. Bill ran as fast as he could to get to the car, and luckily, Preston's life was saved that day. Wow! What an experience that was. I did not yell at Preston for leaving my side. I knew it was my fault for not keeping an eye on him. All I could do was just grab him and hold him tight. Preston was a very active boy, and you had to watch every step that he took. This incident just proved to me that life was too short and precious and needed to be handled with care. Preston was the center of my world, and I just could not imagine what my life would be like without him.

Preston at church function.

Baptism at St Paul's Church.

God Father's Fred Bray and Bill Crosky.

Chapter 5

Preston loved to do dangerous things that I guess most boys his age do. Most of the people I spoke to that had boys told me that boys were daredevils and would do things that girls would not even dream of doing. I guess I was getting it firsthand with my son.

I remember one weekend; Preston was making all kinds of shapes with Play-Doh. Somehow or another the Play-Doh ended up in Preston's ear. His ear was all infected, and I had to take him to the emergency room to have it removed. The long tube that the doctor stuck into his ear apparently really bothered him. Preston let out this bloodcurdling scream and would not let the doctor put the tube back into his ear. The doctor and nurses had to strap him down to the bed so that they could remove the Play-Doh. Preston was like the Incredible Hulk that day. His little chest became so enlarged, and little veins popped out from his neck. He kept screaming and wriggling around, so the doctor decided that he could no longer complete the task. He told me to follow up with Preston's primary-care doctor to see what he could do. This was horrible. Preston was in so much pain, and I never in my life saw him act out in this way. My heart hurt for him, and I kept hoping his own doctor would have better luck in removing the Play-Doh.

Preston and I left the emergency room, and I followed up as quickly as I could to make him an appointment. The day finally arrived for me to take him in. I don't know exactly what this doctor did different from the emergency-room doctor, but he successfully removed the Play-Doh. Preston was so relieved, and so was I. The doctor prescribed him some medication for an infection and told me to give him some Tylenol for the pain and fever. Preston never did play with any more Play-Doh after that. I learned as a mother that kids do the strangest things and you wonder at times exactly how some of these things happen.

Another incident that showed me how active boys are had to do with a miniature pool table I'd bought for Preston and Joey. While playing, one of the small balls got stuck in Joey's nose. Joey had to be transported to the hospital. I do not know for the life of me what the two boys were thinking when they did these things. These two boys were a lot of fun, but they never ceased to amaze me. I guess the life of being a mother is never dull. At least in my case it wasn't. Life was exciting and scary at times, but looking back, I would not trade it for anything in the world.

Preston loved watching football games on television, so imagine how excited he was when Jay, a friend I'd met through Bill, asked if he could take Preston to see our local football team play one weekend. I gave permission and was pleased that Preston would get such a fun opportunity. Later, though, I found out that I could have lost my son that day. Apparently, Jay was buying something for them to eat and drink and thought Preston was right next to him. He was shocked to turn around to see that Preston was nowhere to be found. There were thousands of people at that game. Before long the police at the front gate were dispatched by radio, and about a half hour later, they finally found him at another gate talking to some girls. The thought of all the things that could have happened to my little boy confirmed that he would not be going to any more games unless he was with me or at least a little older. Without a doubt, Preston was a boy that kept me, as well as everyone else on their toes, and I was not about to lose him. At this point, I thought I should get Preston involved in some active sport since he had all this energy. I started taking him over to the Buena Vista School playground not too far from where we lived, and we played baseball and kickball. We rounded up a few boys from the neighborhood, and I let them play until their little bodies tired out and they could play no more. The children appeared to like the sport and enjoy themselves. They never seemed to tire. We continued doing this every chance we could, and it was a good thing for all of us. We were out in the fresh air, and it gave us something constructive to do. Preston and I did not have a yard to play in, so the playground was the perfect place for us to go and have some fun.

I loved these years watching Preston and the other boys. I was like a child myself, and we had so much fun. He was growing up so fast before my eyes, and seeing him having fun gave me so much joy. I wanted him to stay little forever. My precious little boy was going to be four years old soon. I figured that if I could keep him involved with sports that I would never have to worry about him getting into trouble, and this was important to me. These years were vital in his development, and having him in sports meant I never had to worry about him running around the neighborhood or getting into trouble. I felt secure in always knowing where he was.

After seeing an ad in the local paper, I enrolled him in weekly T-ball. I remember the first time he tried to hit the ball. It was the cutest thing. He would swing the bat with all his might and would miss the ball. Preston would get upset when this happened, and each time he went to swing, he would make this face, and I would just laugh. He was so serious and wanted to hit the ball so badly. Now, all the children there were cute in the way they swung the bat. I wish I'd had a video camera for these moments. They all were so precious to watch. I loved seeing how Preston would handle sports in general. These years were the years that were important, and to see him like this was a real joy for me as a mother.

The time finally came for all the children to be on a team, and their first game was not a success. Preston was not happy about this and did not want to play anymore. I explained to him that his first game not being a success did not mean that the other games would be bad as well. I also explained that once we joined something, we never quit. I said that we keep doing it and practicing till we get better and this was the way to perfect everything we do in our lives. He did not agree with me, but we continued to go. Preston soon learned that what I was telling him all along about practicing was paying off. His team started winning games, and Preston gained the confidence to want to play. Preston was beginning to understand that though his team did not always win, that did not mean that he had to quit and feel discouraged. All that really mattered was for him to have fun.

Now, some of the coaches that I've run across did not share these beliefs, and this really affected me. These coaches would have an effect on Preston's mind, and everything I was trying to teach him was taking a backseat to what the coaches were teaching. I never once backed down on the way I explained the sport to Preston. I kept telling him that all he needed to do was to have fun. Preston was still very young. To feel pressure to win from a coach was just not what I wanted for Preston. To me playing sports for fun and not for winning was a good thing to teach him.

I taught Preston that just being the kind and gentle spirit that he was and treating people right made him a winner. Life to me was not about winning the game. I wanted to teach Preston something he enjoyed doing, and if in doing so the team won, well that was just icing on the cake. To me I was teaching Preston that life was not all about winning. I wanted this to sink into his brain so that he would want to continue with an activity even if he lost sometimes. Life to me was so short, and for him to think that he had to win at everything would prove nothing in the grand scheme of things. Preston enjoyed that year playing, and I enjoyed watching him play.

I signed Preston up for the Steubenville Striders track team when he turned five years old. He had so much energy and seemed to like running, so why not try him at this sport? Preston really did well in this. They had to do exercises just like the ones for the high school students. Preston had a little trouble at first learning to do the squats, stretching exercises, and jumping jacks. I would just stand there smiling. He had an awkward way of doing his exercises, with his body movements out of sync. After he was finished running, he would come to me and say, "Mom, I really do not like this." He wanted to quit, so we again had the conversation about not quitting once we've started something. He did not like it but finished up the year winning a trophy. I told him all his hard work had paid off and that I was proud of him for sticking it out. I honestly think that he was never so happy for the season to end. He never did join track again after that year, but he was getting a real taste for the different types of sports available to him.

Preston and his neighborhood buddies would still play baseball and kickball, which appeared to be the sports that Preston enjoyed the most. Preston had quite the arm on him when it came to throwing a ball. He surprised me for a boy of his age. He could throw a lot farther than most of the boys his age. I was thinking I had a real Babe Ruth on my hands. Not really, but it was wonderful to see him enjoy playing a sport. I enrolled him for baseball tryouts that year. Tryouts consisted of the boys throwing the ball to each other, swinging the bat, running around the baseball field, and hitting the ball to see how far it would go. The coaches watched and picked the boys that they wanted on their teams. Preston was chosen to be on the Angels.

The Angels had practice once a week starting out, and the coach was hard on all the boys at first. This coach was very serious about the game and wanted the children to have fun but also win. At practices, I watched from the sidelines. The coach initially chose Preston for the outfield. Preston was the first one to get the ball and throw it in. The team was quite impressed with how fast the ball made it in, and the coach kept Preston in the outfield for a while. The time came when it was Preston's turn to bat, and the coach was impressed with how far Preston could hit the ball. Preston was a serious hard hitter, but when he ran to the base, he would get tagged out. Preston would get very upset over this. The coach tried to encourage him and let him know that he was doing a great job and that it may not always be like this.

When the first practice ended, Preston told me he wanted to be the pitcher. I told him that this was only the beginning and to stick it out because he just might get picked to be the pitcher later. Preston liked baseball, and he seemed to want to do everything all at once. I explained to him that in time things just may turn around and that if they did; he should do his best with what was given to him.

While he was in sports, some emotional issues started to crop up. Preston asked me questions about where his dad was. I told him that when his father, Mike, and I were together, I had other obligations to tend to, and so his dad and I could not be together. I always said the nicest things about his father because I did not want to sway his thinking. I told him his dad, wherever he was, loved him very much and that it just was not a good time for us to be together. This appeared to ease his mind a bit, but I could still see Preston's yearning for his father. He wanted to know more about his father. On all his sports teams the other kids' fathers were present. I think this is what raised questions for him, but at the time, I didn't give it much thought. I felt such anguish in my heart for Preston to see all the fathers with their sons while not having his father close by. I told him that I would try to locate his father even though I had no idea where in the world Mike was.

Chapter 6

I always encouraged Preston and told him that the important thing in sports was to enjoy the game. Baseball practice seemed to last months before they started playing games. Two months before their first game, the coach started holding daily practices. The times were grueling. They practiced from five to nine o'clock at night. This really took a toll on Preston. When they were finished, he went home and slept. I thought nothing could tire my son out, but this actually did the trick.

The boys practiced nonstop for two months, and then they played their first game. Preston was learning just how hard you had to work at something if you really wanted it. Their first game was a real success, and they won. The coach treated the whole team with pizza. Preston became MVP for most of the games that year. He won several trophies that he proudly displayed in his bedroom. The whole team was excited and happy that they were successful and won many games. The season eventually ended, and it could not have been more pleasurable than what it was.

I next enrolled Preston in soccer. To my amazement, he excelled in this as well. He would kick the ball into the net with lightning speed. I loved going and watching my son. The faces that he made when kicking showed how serious he was about the sport. I was excited to see Preston grow up right before my eyes. The time finally came to enroll him in kindergarten at Buena Vista School. The school was about three blocks from our home, so Preston did not need to ride the bus. We walked to and from school daily.

We went the first day to meet his teacher, Mrs. Johnson. She was a sweet woman and had a soft voice. She told Preston and me all the fun things that he would be doing during the year. Preston took a liking to her right off the bat and kept asking questions about what he would need and where he would sit. Preston appeared to enjoy that year. He received all check marks on his report card, and Mrs. Johnson always had nice things to say about him. Preston became friends with a boy named Anthony. The two of them got along well with one another and became the best of friends. That year they spent a lot of time together and wanted to play at each other's homes, so I would often drive Preston to Anthony's house and then pick Preston up when it was time to come home.

That year ended, and Preston and Anthony graduated to the first grade and were placed in Mrs. Newman's class. Preston and Anthony were still the best of friends. They decided that they wanted to walk to school together. We lived in a nice, quiet neighborhood, and I saw no problem with this. Anthony would walk to our home, and from there, he and Preston would go to school. My son was becoming his own independent person and growing away from me.

Preston came to me one day and asked if he could join karate with Anthony. I asked him if he understood what karate was all about. I don't think he understood the whole concept, so I explained to him what I knew. We discussed what he should and should not do in karate. I told him that karate was only to be used in the line of defense. If his life was in danger, he could use this. He assured me that he understood, so I enrolled him in the class.

I loved watching him learn about his kicks and his stances and loved hearing him say *KIA* as he did each kick. Preston's teacher reinforced what I told Preston about karate being used only when defending oneself and not to harm anyone. So I was surprised when I learned that Preston had used a karate move on Anthony when they were walking to school one morning. Anthony got hurt, and I reprimanded Preston for this. That was the end of karate for Preston. He was not happy, but I explained to him that if Anthony had been hurt more and had to go to the hospital, the outcome would not have been good. Preston and Anthony still played together and were the best of friends, but karate was no longer a part of Preston's life.

Preston and Anthony were great students and excelled in every subject. They both made the honor roll, and I could not have been a prouder mother. Preston was academically progressing, and I thanked the Lord for all the guidance that I had given to Preston since birth. I finally realized that I must be doing something right and thanked God for this reward. Seeing Preston doing so well made me so happy. Our lives appeared to be shaping up for what God had given us, and I was grateful for all the love that was bestowed upon us at this time. We continued to go to church, and this time in our lives was peaceful.

The year ended, and Preston graduated to the second grade. He was on the honor roll again. He was my little scholar and doing so well. The next year went without a hitch, and he graduated to the third grade with high honors. He was way above average and again excelled in every subject. One of our rules was that Preston had to do his homework before he could go out to play. I had to do this growing up, so I did this with my son. He never did like this idea, but I explained to him that he would have more time to play if he did this. This policy worked out well for us. He never had to really study very long because his mind soaked, everything up like a sponge. I would question him on his homework, and he always amazed me.

One time I said, "You know, Son, I was never fortunate like you." I asked him if he realized how blessed he was. I told him how I had to really read and reread everything in order for it to soak into my brain. I let him know how proud I was of him and what a true gift from God he was.

He just smiled at me and said, "Yes, Mom, I know."

I laughed and said, "You are such a modest boy."

Preston and I had a special relationship that most kids his age probably did not have with their mothers. I not only was his mother but a true friend as well. We spent a lot of time together and learned many things about each other. This bond could never be broken, and I felt blessed. The school year ended, and Preston once again was on the honor roll and was promoted to the fourth grade. He spent the summer again playing baseball and soccer. Anthony even came to a few of his games to cheer him on.

Not long after this Preston met a boy from our neighborhood through another friend. Preston wanted to go to this boy's home, but I didn't know anything about this boy or where he lived exactly. I found out the boy lived a block down the street from us, so I went down and introduced myself. I told the man that answered the door that my son and his son wanted to play together and that I wanted to make sure that it was okay with him. The boy's father told me his name was Clyde and invited me inside. We sat and had a nice visit. He was divorced and had custody of his two sons and was raising them single like me. He was interested in working out and had some workout equipment in his basement. He asked if I wanted to give it a try. I had never worked out much with weights before but told him I would try. We worked out a little bit and then exchanged telephone numbers before saying our good-byes.

I didn't realize it at the time, but I later found out that Clyde knew my son's family. It is a funny world we live in, how everything falls into place just when we need it the most. This man's son and Preston continued to play that summer, and they became the best of friends.

Clyde called me up one day and invited me over, and we had a nice chat about Preston's father, Mike. I was stunned to learn that Mike's sister was married to Clyde's brother. How ironic was that! Clyde told me that his brother's marriage didn't work out and told me he would help me in contacting Mike's sister. He gave me her telephone number, but before he did, he made me promise that I would not tell her how I got her number. I promised but wondered how in the world I was going to call someone out of the clear blue sky and tell her that her brother was my son's father and that I was trying to locate him. How was I going to explain how I got her number? I didn't know. I was relieved and scared at the same time. This whole situation was freaky. I just hoped in my heart that when I did make the call everything would work out the way Preston's heart wanted. I did not call her right away. I was a little apprehensive as to what I would exactly say. My whole body was shaking from hearing this news. I rehearsed in my mind several times before I decided to call.

I finally got up enough nerve one day to make the call. I explained to her who I was and how her ex-brother-in-law had given me her telephone number. I don't know if she ever told Clyde about me calling her or not. She was furious, but she still listened to me as I told her about how Preston was a part of her family. She said she hadn't spoken to her brother for a while, and from what I gathered, she was not pleased with him at all. I asked her if I sent her pictures and my telephone number if she would forward them to her brother. I also asked if she would claim Preston as part of the family. She told me she would not until Preston's father would. I could not blame her for this, because I was a total stranger to her and calling her up and telling her this news was strange, I'm sure. She gave me her address, and we said our good-byes. I got off the phone that day and was so hurt in how the conversation went. While deciding whether to send the pictures and my telephone number, I could only hope that something good would come out of this. Around this time, I found out that the rent for our apartment was being raised. I asked our proprietor why the rent was going up, and he said that the houses across the street were going to be moved to a new location and a highway was going to be built on our street. I did not see how that should affect us, but because of the raised rent, we would have to move. How sad that was, to leave the apartment we had come to love. It was painful and devastating to know that we were once again searching for a home. I went the next day to the local stores and bought a paper and collected boxes for the new journey that was about to begin.

Chapter 7

I started to look at other places to live. I no longer worked at the country club and was receiving government assistance until I could get Preston and myself on our feet. I searched the market to see what was available but could find nothing to fit our budget. I applied and had an interview at the Fort Steuben low-income housing that was located in Wintersville, Ohio. They had a vacant apartment available but had to run a background check on me and needed to complete some improvements on the apartment before they could let us move in. I left there that day feeling like such a failure. I did not want to raise Preston up in this type of environment at all. I was thinking that it was going to be like the movie *Bates Motel.* You can check in but never check out. I continued to look and pray for something better but to no avail: I found nothing.

About a month and a half later, I received something in the mail from the housing authorities telling me that I could move in. I was never so distraught in all my life. My faith at this time was not good, and I could think only of the worst things that could happen. Preston and I packed up all our belongings and left for the Bates Motel. I will never forget the day we moved in. I cried so hard because all I wanted to do was to give Preston the best possible life I could, and moving here was not it.

Our apartment was spacious with two bedrooms, kitchen, dining room, living room, vanity with a sink and mirror, bathroom, and a front window that looked out over a parking lot. I asked myself, "Is this the view that we have to look forward to?" I could find no beauty in this place at all. The apartment building had two floors, and our apartment was on the top floor. I knew from speaking with people that lived there that there was no privacy. You could hear when your next-door neighbor went to the bathroom and when parents reprimanded their children. I wanted a peaceful and calm atmosphere. I wanted to leave the same day we moved in but had nowhere else to go. I tried within my heart to find some kind of beauty in this move. I started unpacking things, and Preston helped as best he could. I had a set of beautiful curtains that provided me some beauty.

As the days progressed, we got acclimated to the surroundings, and it started to look like a place that we could actually live, at least for a little while anyway. Preston wanted to go outside and meet other boys to play with. I wasn't comfortable or familiar with the children in this neighborhood. I wanted to protect him from the harm that I thought was out there. I finally let him go outside, and he met three boys who lived there. This was not a good experience for him at all. One of the boys started to bully him, which upset Preston. I asked him which boy was bulling him, and I walked right up to the boy and asked him what the problem was. I told him that bullying was not a way to handle friendship. The bullying continued for about three weeks or so, and since my conversation with the boy did not work, I thought I should visit with his parents. I found out where the boy lived and went straight up to the door and knocked on it. The boy's mother answered the door. I let her know that we were new to the neighborhood and that her son was bullying Preston. The conversation went well, and she assured me that she would talk to her son.

The next day, Preston wanted to ride his bike, a gift from a friend of ours, and I told him to be careful riding it around the parking lot so that he did not get hit by someone pulling in or out of the lot. He assured me that he would be careful. After he was out there for only about twenty minutes, I looked out to check on him, and he was nowhere in sight. I walked away from the window, and he knocked at our door to get back in. He told me that the boys he was playing with took his bike and he could not get it back. I was livid. I could not believe this. This kind of behavior was what I had been protecting him from all along. This proved to me more each day that we should not be living here. Preston was crying and all upset, and I clearly realized that we were dealing with boys who had no respect for other people or their things.

"Who did this to you?" I asked. I found out it was the same boy who had been bullying him. I marched myself right up to the boy once again and told him to return the bike or I would press charges on him for stealing. The boy yelled a few cuss words at me, and I could not believe what I was hearing him say. I knew it was Preston's first time hearing someone cuss. I never spoke to Preston like that, and if he had ever spoken to me in that manner, I would've washed his mouth out with soap. I again had a conversation with the boy's mother, and she said she would solve the problem. The mother explained to me that her son was having some issues with his dad being in prison and that she was having behavioral problems with him as a result. I sympathized with her and told her how sorry I was but said her son should not be cussing or treating other children in this manner. She agreed with me and said she had her son in counseling but that it wasn't working. I told her Preston was a very sensitive boy and was not used to someone treating him like this. I also told her to let me know if there was anything I could do to help.

That night before going to sleep, Preston and I both said prayers for this boy and wondered what we could do to help. The next day I suggested to Preston that we bring this boy over to our house for a visit. Preston asked him over, and he did come. The boy appeared a little apprehensive in coming over, and I'm sure he was wondering why we wanted him there. I had a purpose for this visit. When the boy showed up, I welcomed him in. I had baked cookies that morning and had some milk out and offered him some. I was very pleasant and made sure he felt welcomed.

We spoke awhile about how long he had lived there, and I asked him if he was happy about where he lived. The boy liked living there and had been there for quite some time before Preston and I had moved in. I asked him if he had ever been to church. He said he hadn't. I then asked him if he'd like to attend a Bible study I'd be having in my home. I told him we would love to have him if he wanted to come. Well, I don't know if anyone had ever approached this boy in this manner before or not, but calmness appeared to come over him. He seemed to want to stay and visit. Preston showed him his bedroom, his entire trophy collection, and some of the pictures on his wall. The boy appeared to be interested in what Preston showed him and what Preston had done in his life. I thought that just maybe they were going to have a nice friendship after all. Preston received his bike back, and we started to have Bible study once a week in our home. Five boys would attend, and we all had fun.

I not only held Bible study for these boys, but we also would do little skits on worldly things that I thought would be important for them later on in life. I pretended I was a drug dealer and tried to sell each of them drugs so they could work on their responses in situations like this. I thought these little skits would teach them valuable lessons. Preston became very popular with the boys in the apartment complex, and I tried to help in the friendships when I could. Our life was becoming somewhat peaceful, and Preston appeared to be happy with the boys he was meeting.

One day he brought a new boy, Mike, in to visit. Mike was the cutest little boy. He had brown hair and freckles on his face. When he spoke, his vocabulary was like that of an adult. Mike was a little bit like a professor and came up with all kinds of things that most kids his age would not even dream up. This intrigued me, and I wanted to know more about what was inside this little professor's mind. He would come up with ways to make money and encouraged Preston to look for things that he had and wanted to sell. Mike's idea was that they would then use the money to buy pop at the pop machine located outside of the complex. How ingenious this was for a boy of his little stature to contemplate. I thought this would teach them they had to sell something in order to receive something and teach them the value of a dollar. Preston would no longer have to come to me and ask me for something. He could earn it and appreciate how he came to get it. I thought this was fantastic. Preston and Mike became inseparable, the best of friends. The other boys still wanted to play with Preston, but something different was forming between Preston and Mike.

Mike had this magnifying glass that he carried around with him. He reminded me of a little Inspector Gadget. On one particular day, Preston had done something wrong, so I would not let him go outside to play. As punishment, I kept him inside that day. I decided to go to the store, and I gave Preston the keys to the car to go sit inside until we could leave. I came down from our apartment and saw him sitting on the bench in front of our apartment. Preston gave me the keys, and I got in and started the car. I smelled something burning and asked Preston what it was. He said he didn't know. I searched the car and tried to figure out where the smell was coming from. I finally opened the glove box, and it was engulfed with smoke. I put the fire out with some rags from the backseat.

I looked at Preston and asked, "How did this happen?" He again said he didn't know. About this time, Mike came walking across the parking lot with his magnifying glass, and Preston told me that Mike had started it. The sun was blazing outside that day, and I could see how this could have happened. I knew if you used a magnifying glass to direct sunlight onto something long enough that a fire could start. I got out of the car, approached Mike, and explained to him what Preston said he had done. Mike assured me that he was not the one who did it and was sorry to hear what had happened. I scolded Preston and told him I wanted the truth and to turn over to me what had started the fire. Preston handed me a set of matches that he had found in the glove box, and I told him to apologize to Mike for lying. I told Mike that Preston would not be allowed to play with him that day, and we proceeded on to the store.

I had a long talk with Preston while we drove, and I asked him why he did this. He was angry at being grounded, and this was his way of expressing his anger. I told him about the importance of not starting fires and grounded him for a week for lying. Preston was not a happy camper that day. The glove box was completely melted from the fire he'd started, and I kept thinking about how I was going to come up with the money to fix this problem. I kept Preston busy with things around the house during that week, and he kept trying to get me to give in on the grounding. I told him that this was a serious matter and that what I set was going to stay in place.

The week finally passed, and I let Preston go outside to play. Before letting him go, I asked him what he had learned about being punished. He expressed to me the importance of not starting fires and expressed how sorry he was for lying about his friend. He added that he would never do that again.

Preston and Mike continued to play, and they had another close friend named TJ that would join them from time to time. The boys liked playing in the woods down over the hill from where we lived. Mike told me that one time when they were in the woods, he and Preston had found a baby deer. Mike thought it was precious and wanted to keep it, so he took it home. His mother, Nancy, thought it was beautiful but told Mike they could not keep it, and so she returned the deer to the woods. Mike and Preston were always finding animals, birds, and rabbits and would come home and tell me all about them.

These two boys came up with all sorts of things to do. Some were good and some not so good. They would take walks to Canella's Market and buy Airheads at five cents apiece. You can't buy candy for that amount today. The boys would come up with ways to make money and then splurge on things they wanted. After buying the things that they wanted, they would always return to the woods to a crab apple tree to eat as if they were camping out.

Chapter 8

Preston and Mike were having the time of their lives playing together. They loved playing the Mortal Kombat video games and sleeping over at one another's home. They were becoming like brothers, and nothing besides getting grounded or going to school separated them. Mike was a little younger than Preston, and Mike told me that Preston taught him how to tie his shoes. He said that it was hard for him to learn, but when Preston showed him, it was easy. Mike would play pranks on Preston just to see how he would react to them.

Mike told me about a time he asked Preston, "You think you can tackle me?" Preston held out both of his hands and ran toward Mike. Mike then put his foot out and tripped Preston. I had been wondering where Preston picked this up. One time Preston was sitting on a bench outside, and I watched from our picture window as he deliberately put his foot out and tripped one of the boys walking by. The boy fell, and I marched my way down the stairs and hollered for Preston to come inside. I could not believe what I had just witnessed. I was fit to be tied. I scolded him and asked him what in the world he was doing. I explained that it was not a laughing matter and told him the child he tripped could have seriously gotten hurt. Preston apologized to me, and I told him to go apologize to the child at once. The child accepted his apology, but Preston was grounded for the rest of the day. I did not realize it at the time, but Mike was teaching Preston some unacceptable behaviors. Preston was old enough and should have known better, but Mike was not helping matters at all.

Mike looked up to me, and I tried my best to teach him the same morals that I was teaching Preston. Mike was like my own. He was a part of our family. I did not mind this at all. I could see how close Mike and Preston were, and I did not want this to end. This friendship seemed to be a good thing for Preston. The more I had the two of them in my home, the more secure I felt, because I could monitor everything they did. The two of them were not bad kids; they were just being boys. I had a lot of fun with both of them.

When the boys were not outside playing, they would come inside, and we would play all kinds of board games together. Preston and Mike enjoyed Monopoly. It was a good game to play and took a long time to complete. Preston would always try to cheat, and Mike would always call him on this. While Preston and Mike were enjoying their game, I would often cook them one of their favorite meals or make pizza and bake cookies. I loved to cook, and the boys enjoyed eating. My entertainment consisted of listening to music, cleaning the house, shopping, reading books, taking walks with my girlfriend, going to church, and spending time with my boyfriend at the time, Jay.

I struggled with the thought of raising Preston without my biological family. I knew from my experience in many foster homes that extended family was important. My siblings and I were not close and were separated from one another throughout our lives growing up. We did not have any contact with one another until later on in our lives. I think that if they'd had the chance to participate in our lives a little more that our lives would have been a lot easier. I loved family and would always try to include mine in whatever we did, but they seemed to have other things going on in their lives. If I could change anything from these years, it would be to have my family around more.

Right around this time I took it upon myself to send the pictures and my telephone number to Preston's father's sister. I did not receive anything in the mail as the days and months passed. I did not tell Preston about sending the pictures and number because I did not know how to explain to him if his father did not respond. All we had was a prayer and a hope to go on. The summer ended, and Preston returned to school. Fifth grade that year went well, and Preston passed and graduated to the sixth grade and again was on the honor roll. Mike and Preston would meet and walk every morning to the bus stop, which was located at the end of the road right at the entrance of the complex. They, along with other boys and girls, would always walk in pairs. This seemed safe and worked out well for them.

Preston was doing quite well in the beginning. Then about the middle of the year, I received a paper in the mail about Preston not being in school on certain days. The school did not make phone calls to check up on the children like when I was in school. I had a conversation with Preston about this because I knew the days in question were not days that he had been sick and he should have been at school. I found out that he and a boy he met in school had been skipping school and hanging out in the woods. I expressed to him how important it was for him to have his education and asked him why he was skipping school. Preston told me that he was bored and felt he already knew what the teacher was teaching. I told him that no matter what he felt, he still had to attend. Preston was always a little bit farther in his education than most of the children in his class, and everything came easy for him. I told him that in order for him to get what he wanted out of life; he had to stay in school. I expressed to him that he had to end his friendship with the boy he skipped school with and that this type of behavior was not acceptable. I could not believe this coming from my child. I was trying to do my best in raising him, and for him to do something like this just tore my heart to pieces. I had no control over him once he left my home, and I prayed that this behavior would cease.

As the days passed, I watched him closely and realized that he did not want to do his homework or anything that I tried to get him to do. He started becoming defiant with me. I could not for the life of me understand this behavior whatsoever. He started smarting off to me, and at times, I felt as if I had no control over him. I would have plenty of conversations with him and gave him the ground rules that he had to follow, but this, along with grounding, was not working. I enrolled him into counseling sessions. My baby was slipping away from me, and I could not help him. I wondered about everything that was happening in our lives about this time. I started losing hope and blaming it on myself for putting us into this situation of living where we were. I did not know why all this was happening, but I needed answers and a quick solution.

I set up an appointment with his homeroom teacher and found out that he was hanging around the wrong kind of children. Apparently, these children were not being guided in the right direction at home. The teacher told me that his grades were slipping and that if they were not brought up, she would have to fail him for that semester. I asked if he could make up the work that he'd missed.

She told me that the semester was going to end soon and that Preston would really have to buckle down and get it handed in before the semester ended. I told her that all she needed to do was gather up what he had missed and that I would make sure he handed it in on time. This year was grueling for both Preston and me.

Bill had given Preston a nice oak desk that he'd had since his college days. The desk was in Preston's bedroom and was to be used for his homework. One day I walked in to check on him and discovered that instead of using the desk for his homework, he was marking up the sides of the drawer with some sort of sharp object. I cannot for the life of me remember what it was that he had used, but the marks were embedded in the wood. I was not happy with him at all and scolded him for not appreciating the desk. I asked him to hand over to me what he'd used and to explain why he felt he had needed to do this. He told me he was mad and wanted to go outside and play. I told him that if he hadn't skipped school, he would be allowed to enjoy being outside with the other children to play. These were the repercussions for what he'd done. I also told him that the remainder of his schoolwork from that time on would be spent at the kitchen table. He could go outside only after he had completed his homework and I'd checked it. He was not happy about this and started goofing off. I told him the longer he sat there and goofed off, the later it was getting and he would not get to do what he wanted. He would finally finish his homework, but by the time he completed it, it was dark outside and time to go to bed. This continued for the rest of the school year, but Preston did graduate to the seventh grade.

Chapter 9

I never in my life was so exasperated, and I felt that we needed a vacation that year. My boyfriend, Jay, suggested that we go to Myrtle Beach for about a week. We drove my car to cut down cost on airfare. Preston and I looked forward to taking this trip. My son and I had never been on a trip together since the trip to Georgia to see my older brother William and his daughter, Summer. Preston had been three years old then, and how wonderful I thought that trip was.

Preston was excited and started packing up his clothes and everything that he thought he would need for the trip. Preston had a Berea hat that he wore proudly, so he decided to bring it. The trip was going to be long, so I told Preston he could bring some of his handheld games to occupy his time. We finally got on the road for this little getaway trip. I felt as if we would never reach our destination, but we did finally arrive at our hotel that was not far from the beach. We had to walk a block or so to get to the beach, but we did not mind this at all. The sand on the beach was white, and the look on Preston's face was priceless.

I could not contain myself for the joy that my son expressed. His face lit up like a Christmas tree. The weather was nice and warm, and the ocean was as blue as the sky. The waves were not high, and the ocean went on for miles and miles. Seagulls flew above the ocean and beach, and people with boogie boards tried to surf the small waves. Preston could not wait to get into the water. He wanted a boogie board so he could ride the waves. He appeared to enjoy himself, and that made me happy. I had been to many beaches throughout my life, but this was Preston's first. He was excited and wanted to do everything at once. Jay and I bought him a boogie board. I knew this was going to be a sight to see. Preston grabbed the boogie board so fast and headed for the water. He tried to ride the small waves that were coming in, but they were too slow. He went to climb on the board before the waves came in and fell off. I enjoyed watching him try to get the hang of it.

Preston loved the water and wanted to walk the pier that appeared to go on for miles in the distance. We reached the pier and walked up to the ledge where people were fishing. Preston saw his first live shark and could not contain himself. The sharks were close to the pier, and people were catching them with fishing poles. Preston wanted to catch one, but Jay and I said we would just stand and watch. I thought if I let him fish that one of those sharks would pull him over the pier. That would not have been a good sight for me to see. I told Preston that we would like to have him around for a while rather than him being a shark's dinner.

We continued down the beach, and Jay and I found a spot to sit down and soak up the hot sun while we watched Preston swim and enjoy himself. This was one of the most memorable times of our lives. It was wonderful. Preston was like a little kid in the water and kept swimming around and trying to do handstands. Evening came, and we went and got a bite to eat. Preston wanted to know what else there was to do. There was a carnival down the road with lots of rides, and Preston was excited to go.

We finished up our dinner and headed for the carnival. There was this bungee-type thing that went into the air, and Preston said, "Mom, come and go on that." I was always afraid of things like that that hung in the air. I told him it scared me to death and that I did not think I would be flying in the air. Preston was a real daredevil, and he didn't seem at all afraid of trying it. We paid the man, and I watched as they hooked him up to these long cords. Preston was all fastened in and ready to go. This big machine hoisted him up and pulled him into the sky. I looked on in amazement and thought, *No one could ever get me to fly into the air like that.* Preston hollered down at me, and then the cord let loose, and he went flying through the air. I was so sure the cord was going to break. Preston flew down and came close to where I was standing, or at least it seemed that way. I just stood there in total panic as my heart raced. Preston screamed and yelled. He was having a blast, and I could not believe that he was enjoying this. He flew in the air for what seemed like forever and then was hoisted off. He said he had fun and that Jay and I must try it. We both shook our heads no and continued walking around the park.

I was never fond of roller coasters or for that matter anything that put me high away from the ground. I stayed away from those rides. Preston and Jay rode the roller coaster as I watched from the ground. They put their hands in the air and laughed and screamed at the top of their lungs. That night we stayed up to the wee hours of the morning and then went back to the motel.

The following day Preston went to the shops alongside the street from our motel. Jay gave him some money, and we set a time for us to meet. Jay and I soaked up the sun on the beach and waited for Preston to return. When Preston returned, he was so excited and started telling us about this wonderful haunted house he'd visited. He said we should check it out. Preston was fond of anything that scared you. It intrigued him. He was a prankster, and seeing those things gave him creative ideas that he could use for Halloween. I took pictures of us while we were on vacation, and this captured precious memories for life. Spending quality time with family and doing things together was important for me. I wanted this to last forever and hoped this trip would get Preston back on track with his studies.

The week finally ended, and it was time to go home. The trip on the way back was horrible. It was hot and muggy, and the air conditioner was not cooling us down. I did not know how we were going to make it in a hot car. We were stuck in traffic that appeared to be backed up for miles. I don't think I have ever witnessed this much traffic in all my life. Jay, Preston, and I wondered where everyone was going to or coming from. We were hungry and thirsty, and the car needed gas. We wondered how long it would take to get to the nearest gas station.

We finally reached a gas station and got gas and something to eat. Jay put some of his food on top of the compartment box that was between the seats. Preston decided to rest his feet on this, and Jay got upset. He scolded Preston and would not allow Preston to eat because of this. I asked Preston to move his feet and told Jay that we were all going to eat our food. I thought this was out of character and extreme of Jay. The rest of the trip home was silent. I don't know whether the heat coming from outside was causing this crankiness, but I knew it was one of the most miserable trips back home I'd ever had.

When we finally arrived home, we went straight to bed from pure exhaustion. Preston had a couple of days before starting school, and this gave us both the time we needed to unwind from the trip. Preston returned to school, and if I remember correctly, things were going quite well for a little while. Preston was still hanging out with the wrong kids at school, and I had to figure out a way to end this. His grades were picking up, and he did graduate to the eighth grade. This was a relief for me, but his behavior at home was not any better.

I could tell something deeper was going on with my son that he was not expressing to me. He was acting out and showing me signs that I clearly could not figure out. Jay and I would discuss this, and Jay's methods of reprimanding Preston were not like mine at all. I wanted to ground Preston and take things away from him. Jay's methods were harsher and did not seem like a good way to teach my child. Jay's upbringing was not like Preston's, and I felt what worked out for Jay would not necessarily work for my son.

I tried to find a better way to help Preston and figure out what was going on with him. Preston was a sensitive boy and had to be dealt with carefully. I never once while he was growing up spanked him. We had a naughty chair that I used when he was small, and we had conversations about what he did wrong. Usually if you had a conversation with him about what he did, he would turn around and do what was right. This punishment was chosen at his day care center, and it seemed to work. This was how I continued to punish him when he did something wrong. Now that he was older, I'd realized that I'd spared the rod only to spoil my child. These teen years were hard to turn around, and it clearly was too late to spank him. I tried desperately to figure out a way to help my son in whatever it was that was bothering him.

I enrolled him into counseling once more to try to come up with the answers that I clearly did not have. The counseling sessions were scheduled without me at first. I spoke to the counselor in private and found out that Preston was having some trouble dealing with his peers. The counselor said Preston's father not being in his life was an issue. Even though I had tried my best to be a good role model, these issues were all too common among single-parent households. The counselor said he would see what he could do to help the situation. I had expressed my concern about Preston not wanting to go to school and explained that I clearly couldn't leave my job when I had to work. I totally was at my wit's end in trying to find a solution to Preston's problems. Preston was attending Wintersville High School, and this was perfect for what I thought we faced next.

I got a job working at the local Bantam Ridge School not too far from where we lived. This teaching job was set up through the community action council, and I found that I loved it. I ended up taking Preston to and from school every day. Preston joined football that year, and I set up a scheduled time that I would pick him up after school. Preston did not like this, but this way I knew that he was staying in school, and I did not have to worry. Some days I traveled to New Alexander School in Mingo Junction, Ohio, and some days I had to pick Preston up later. I would pick Preston up at the track field, and he was always there when I arrived. Things started to get better, or at least it appeared that way.

Chapter 10

Preston continued his eighth-grade year, and his grades were coming along nicely. A teacher named Mrs. Ensile took an interest in Preston. She saw something special in him and felt he had a lot of potential. She had many discussions with Preston about school and tried her best to give him guidance. That year Mrs. Ensile got sick and passed away. Preston and I both were stunned to hear the news.

He said to me, "Mom, you know she was like no other teacher I ever met. She really liked me."

I told Preston I understood and added, "You will always have the memories of her and what she tried to instill in you. Remember what she gave you, and make her proud of you. She saw something special in you, so don't let her down."

I continued to work for the schools. Preston graduated from eighth grade at Wintersville Middle School and would be attending Big Red High School for ninth grade. I could not believe we'd made it this far. Things were not easy for us up until this point, but I was praising God that we were making progress. I was transferred to Well's School for the Gifted that year; it was a school that Preston was once selected to attend, and was closer to the Big Red High School. When Preston was finished with school, he would walk up to where I was working, and then we would go home together from there. Things appeared to be going great at first.

I was working for minimum wage, and even though I loved my job, the pay was just not enough to make me stay. I wanted more out of life and wanted the best for Preston and me. I started putting in applications for other prospects. I found a job up in Pittsburgh working for a real-estate company as a title representative and had to be at work at seven in the morning. Rescission came in the middle of each month, and I had to work till ten at night at those times. I told Preston that he was going to have to catch the bus until we could make other arrangements for him get to school. I was finally going to be able to move us out of our apartment complex and into a house.

We had a Merchannet paper that came out weekly, and to my surprise, I found a place on a street in my hometown that was not familiar to me. The ad read, "Brick home, located in a nice neighborhood with two bedrooms, nice living room, and rec room, kitchen, with basement, utility room, a garage, and a nice yard." I thought this sounded nice and could not wait to see where it was located. Despite how long I'd lived in Steubenville, I did not know where this place was. I found it was right around the corner from Brady Estates. I called the number, and the place was still vacant. I arranged to see it and met the couple that was renting the home. It was on a corner lot and was perfect. I asked how much the rent was, and to my surprise, I thought I'd be able to afford it. The couple told me that another person was coming to look at it, but they would get back in touch with me. I thanked them for showing me the place and left there on a hope and a prayer. I drove back to the house that night and parked on the side of the street crying for what could be mine. I said another prayer and asked the Lord to open this door for me if it was his will. I was hoping to make this move and have everything work out in my favor.

A week went by and then two. I called and left a message on the couple's answering machine and told them how much I enjoyed looking at their home and how beautiful I thought it was. I finally received a call from them extending the house to me. They seemed like the nicest people I had ever met. I asked if I could paint the walls, because the living room had this red-and-gold-paisley, crush-velvet wallpaper that would not go with my furniture. They told me that the house at one time belonged to one of their parents, who were Italian. They gave me their blessings on painting the walls. They also told me they would lower my rent because I was raising my son as a single mother. I worked so hard for this moment and felt God was blessing Preston and me for all the hardships we'd gone through. I met them once more for the keys to the home, and I hugged them and cried for joy. We were finally in our first home, which I thought was a real achievement after all we had been through.

I continued to work in Pittsburgh, and Preston continued to go to school, or so I thought. I had an alarm clock set for Preston to get up early before I had to leave for work. I would continually have to go in his room and try to get him up, and he would not get up. I told him I could not keep doing this with him and that I could not afford to be late for work. He would lie in his bed as though I hadn't said anything. This went on about three days, and he continued to disobey me and not get up for school.

He still was in counseling, so I told him that if he did not get up and go, I was going to call his counselor. I did not know what else to say to him. I thought that would do the trick. He must have thought I was joking, because he just continued to lie in his bed. I called his counselor who, to my amazement, lived not far from us. I expressed the problems that I was having with Preston not getting up for school and that I had to leave for work. The counselor went way above and beyond the call of duty and came to our home and tried to get Preston out of bed to go to school. I thought we were finished with this phase, but clearly, I was wrong. I told the counselor that I had to leave for work and that I could not stay to make sure he left for school.

I did not know what was going on with my son during this time. I felt blessed and cursed at the same time. My soul cried out for answers that I did not have. The counselor would stay as long as he could to try to get my son up before I left. I reassured the counselor that I would call from work to see if Preston had left. I don't know what I was thinking, because Preston never did answer the phone. I was at my wit's end. Preston had to learn that he was not in charge of his life, and as long as I still had breath in me, he was going to school. I did not care what I had to do to make that happen, but he was going as far as I was concerned. Preston continued to buck me every chance he could. He knew my hands were tied, but there was no way I was going to sign him out from going.

I struggled with this for a while and tried every solution that I thought would work. I finally got fed up one day and called the detention center, and they enrolled him in one of their classes down at the jail. I felt horrible about this but thought it might work out. Preston would see the other side of life when you do not listen to your parents. This detention center was set up for delinquent children who refused to go to school. Their schools sent down homework for them to do. Preston appeared to do well. His completed work was hung up on their wall. The people that worked with him spoke highly of how bright he was. I had no doubt in my mind that he was bright. It was getting him to stay in school that was the problem. Preston just thought that he knew everything there was to know and felt he did not have to go. I was at a loss to understand what was going on with him at the time. I felt as though he was making me pay for something that I had no control over. I could not reach him. Physically and emotionally, I was drained, and this disturbed me. Here was a bright boy, who had his whole life in front of him, and he had something deeply rooted inside him that he was not communicating. He was acting out, and I could not reach him.

While he was going to the detention center, I came up with an idea. I had a foster brother whom Preston was quite fond of, and I suggested that Preston stay with him. My brother lived in another school district, and I thought that maybe Preston would actually go to class if it was a different school. I had a talk with Preston about this idea, and he told me he would go. I arranged a meeting with my brother to take him, and my brother enrolled Preston into the new school district. My brother was working for the police department at the time, and I felt that if Preston got out of hand, my brother would know exactly what to do to set him straight. Preston started going to school and had an after-school job working at a McDonald's. Things appeared to go smoothly.

Then one day after work, my sister-in-law called and told me that Preston was in one of her bedrooms crying and saying he was going to kill himself. I asked her what made him say that, and she said he was having some kind of breakdown or something. I asked her where my brother was, and she told me he was working. The next thing she knew, while she was on the phone with me, Preston darted out her front door. She had to hang up with me to go find him. *Oh my*, I thought. *I better stay here in case he comes here.* Preston was on probation from not going to school, and I knew that if my brother came home and found him not there, Preston was going back to juvenile detention center. This was not good. I tried to remain calm and hope for the best.

Preston did call me, and when he did, I asked him what in the world the problem was. He told me he was not fond of his job at McDonald's and didn't want to go back. I gathered that he and my brother discussed this before my brother left for work and disagreed on the issue. Preston was to go to work that evening, and my sister-in-law called my brother and told him that Preston did not want to go. Preston told me that he wanted to come home. I told him that he could not do that and that my brother would be calling me to see if he was with me. I asked him where he was, just in case my brother did call me. Preston told me he was at a friend's house and that he was leaving and coming home.

I felt so horrible and did not know how to make things better for my son. I of course would let him come home, but I knew in my heart that Preston needed help. At this point nothing we had tried to do for him was working. My brother did call me, and I told him what Preston had said. He told me if Preston did come to my house, I should make him stay there, and my brother would come and pick him up. I knew what my brother was going to do and knew what his obligation to the juvenile authorities were. This was not going as we'd planned, and Preston was making matters worse by not complying with what was expected of him. My brother ended up picking Preston up at his friend's house, and we just waited to see what would happen next.

I continued to go to work every day and had an aching feeling in my stomach that I just could not contain. The last resort for Preston was boot camp. The juvenile authorities and probation officer were notified. The probation officer and I sat down and had a long discussion about Preston not wanting to go to school. I explained that I had Preston stay with my brother to try to help him and had hoped things would change. We all realized that this was not helping. Preston's actions were crying out for some kind of structure that my brother and I could not provide for him at the time. We all were quite baffled at how his potential and his behavior were so mismatched.

Preston went to boot camp in Springfield, Ohio. The unbearable pain I felt in my heart knowing he was going to be that far away from me broke my heart. I remember struggling every day to get up and go to work. I was so used to getting up and having him close by, and now that was not going to happen. All hope seemed to dissipate from me. All I wanted was for my boy to come home and for us to be a happy family.

Preston's boot camp was not how I'd pictured boot camp in my mind or seen on TV. This boot camp was set up living in a regular home, and the school that he went to was a block away. I did not find this out until he was there about a month, but I was relieved to know that the boot camp was in a quiet neighborhood right at the end of the town. They had a basketball court on the side of the house and had some bedrooms that the boys shared. Preston explained to me that three boys stayed in each room, and they slept in bunk beds. They had to do regular chores, like setting the table, washing the dishes, dusting the furniture, and mopping and vacuuming the floors. When they did all that was expected, they were rewarded with things that they wanted to do. They did exercises like the ones in real-life boot camp to keep in shape. The instructor, Mr. Williams, and Preston did not hit it off at first. Mr. Williams told me Preston had an attitude that needed to be adjusted back into shape.

All in all, I was really hoping for the best on this transition even though it was hard on us. I told Preston every time I spoke to him that no matter what we were going through, I would be right there going through it with him. I told him that I loved him very much and all I wanted was for him to do what was expected of him and show them he could be the person I knew in my heart that he could be. Then they would let him come home.

Chapter 11

I went to see Preston every weekend that I could and mailed him things that I knew he would need. We sent letters to each other every week. Leaving after every visit was hard on me. My spirit was weak, and I felt so lonely. I never let him see me cry. I tried my best to be strong for both of us in front of him. When it was time for me to drive home, I would break down and cry. I knew that this was hard on Preston. He had to do things at boot camp that he did not have to do at home. I said a lot of prayers, attended church weekly, and found support through Christian fellowship. I was hoping for the best.

One good thing came out of this: Preston was going to school every day, and this pleased me. I knew his grades were good; I did not have to worry about that. That year Preston graduated with high honors and was inducted into the Who's Who among American High School Students. I was so pleased about this and knew in my heart that when he stayed in school, succeeding was not a problem. Preston graduated to tenth grade that year, and when summer came, he was rewarded with being allowed to go swimming and other activities that the boys wanted to do. The boot camp seemed to be working, and Preston had to earn respect in order to get respect, which was one of the fundamental lessons he would need throughout his life.

I asked Mr. Williams one day how he thought Preston was doing. He said that Preston still needed to work on some things, but he felt Preston could be one of his success stories. He thought that Preston was not a bad kid and just had some things that needed worked on. He felt that things would turn out fine. Mr. Williams thought I did the right thing with Preston and admired how I had raised him as a single parent. He said there were not too many single mothers like me that would take the steps in helping their child as I did. He said that was something to be admired.

I told him how I was raised in and out of the children's home and foster homes and had done the best I could. I told him how my biological mother walked out on me at six years of age. I said that even though my life was not easy raising Preston single, I could never walk out on him as my mother did me. I was going to do my best with whatever means necessary to make him understand that he could become a successful person. I told Mr. Williams I was not perfect and was sure I had made mistakes along the way. But if there was a way to turn this situation around, I was going to do it. I told him that Preston was my world and that I only wanted the best for him. I hoped that what they were instilling in him would last and that he could come home and be the person I always knew in my heart he could be.

Preston joined the wrestling team that year. I do not know if he enjoyed that or not. I think he only joined the sport to get out of the house. The school had a pay phone in their office, and he would call me on it from time to time to see how I was doing and to ask if I was coming up to see him. I always looked forward to hearing from him and going to see him. When 9/11 happened, he called me to see if I was okay. I will never forget that call as long as I live. He was always such a thoughtful boy, and his love and concern for me pleased me so much. I always knew Preston loved me, but I think that Preston had a hard time with not having a father in his life. That tenth-grade year was a great year for Preston.

On one of our calls, he mentioned that he was going to the prom. I asked him if he had a date. He said yes, and I told him I looked forward to getting a picture in the mail. He did send a picture, and he looked so handsome. He had on a hat that looked like something that came out of an Al Capone movie. I believe what my son said in his letter was "The picture was gangster." I don't know where in the world he came up with that, but the picture was a nice one.

Preston graduated that year with high honors and again was inducted into the Who's Who among American High School Students. I once again was proud of him. He was up for a scholarship from Ohio State University. He did not get it, but it was nice to hear that he was a finalist. I was a proud mother indeed. That summer, if all went well, Preston was to come home.

Preston had some activity that Mr. Williams had planned for him to do in a field. I don't recall if it was gardening or what, but whatever it was, Preston did not comply. He said something smart to Mr. Williams, who then notified Preston's probation officer back home, and Preston's privilege of coming home was revoked. They had decided that he would stay there another year, until he turned eighteen. This news saddened my heart. I was so looking forward to him coming home. His attitude was not showing improvement, and my only hope was that keeping him there longer would prove to him that he was not in control of his life. He needed to have some respect for his elders. My son was learning that the school of hard knocks and tough love was not the way to go.

I continued to visit him weekly, and every time I went, he wanted to come home. If Preston complied with all that was asked of him, I was allowed to take him off the property to enjoy our visits together. Preston was taking driver's ed while in school and would ask me to let him drive to our destinations. I would drive a couple of miles away from the facility and pull over and let him drive. This made him happy and seemed to make the visits go a lot smoother. I again would have talks with him during these visits and tell him that as long as he did what was expected of him he would have the privilege of coming home.

Preston had a discussion with Mr. Williams about moving out of the boot camp home and instead living on his own and going to work. Mr. Williams said he would do his part to honor Preston's wishes as long as Preston did what was expected of him. Preston sincerely appeared to want to do the right thing. He must have shown improvement, because in about three months' time Mr. Williams had helped Preston get a job and a place of his own. There were some stipulations, though: Mr. Williams gave Preston a cell phone that Preston would have to pay for, to be used in an emergency or when Mr. Williams needed to call to check on him. Preston had to go to work and come home when finished. Preston would have to attend the rest of his schooling and get himself up every day to go. When he was not working, he had a curfew. Mr. Williams would pay the rent, and all Preston would be responsible for was his food, cleaning supplies, the cell phone, and all other necessities needed to groom himself. This was going to be one of Preston's biggest responsibilities. Mr. Williams wanted to see if Preston could handle it. Preston also was not allowed to have anybody inside the apartment, boy or girl. Mr. Williams honored every one of Preston's wishes and said he wanted to see if Preston could handle being a responsible adult. Preston was given this opportunity because he was reaching a certain age and appeared to want to show how grown up he could be.

I went to visit Preston in his new place. His apartment was small but had all the accommodations that he would need to live. The living room, kitchen, and bathroom were clean, but he wouldn't let me see his bedroom. I knew that when his bedroom door was closed, the room probably wasn't clean. His job was a couple of blocks away, and he could walk to work. I thought he'd improved a lot, and I was proud of him for becoming the person that I knew he could be. I cried because it brought me back to when he was little. I knew in my heart that he was becoming the young man that I had tried so desperately to reach at one time. I was sad and proud at the same time. My boy was growing up. I felt good about myself for helping my boy become responsible for what I knew he had in him. I tried my best to be optimistic at this time and not wonder if he was going to backslide. I always hoped for the best. I felt comfortable in going to work every day. Knowing that my son was doing well gave me a secure feeling and made me proud.

I went to visit him one weekend and found that he was not at home. I went to his job and found him working. He worked the drive-through window at a taco place. I sat down in the closest seat I could find and watched him work until he had to close. My son had a good boss who gave him the responsibility of opening and closing the store. I thought, *He is showing great progress to be given such a responsibility.* Preston appeared to get along well with his boss and his coworkers. They all looked up to him and appreciated him for the job he was doing. I did not know this at the time, but I found out later that Mr. Williams and Preston's boss were best friends. Preston did well that summer, and as time went on, his self-esteem started to improve because of his accomplishments.

The summer ended, and it was time for him to go back to school. He was in the eleventh grade now, and this year was going to be the ultimate test. He had to go to school, do his homework, and go to work. Things were going well in the beginning, and then something happened about the middle of the school year. I found out through Mr. Williams that Preston was not answering his phone. Mr. Williams said he would drive over to Preston's apartment and Preston would not be there. He also drove to Preston's work site, and Preston was absent from his job too. Mr. Williams could not figure out where Preston would go.

One evening, Mr. Williams decided to camp out on the side of the street where Preston lived. He found Preston walking late at night with a few boys past his curfew. He called Preston over and reprimanded him for doing what he knew he shouldn't be doing. Mr. Williams spoke to Preston's boss and found out that Preston was not at work that day and that the responsibility of opening the store had been taken from him. Preston once again failed to prove his accountability for being on his own, and his apartment and phone rights were taken away. This was not good, and Preston had to move back into the boot camp. I felt horrible hearing this news and did not know what else we could do to help my son. This boot camp was the last resort, and everything that was going on at this time seemed hopeless.

Right around this time, I lost my job working for the real-estate company in Pittsburgh. I loved my job, and their reason for letting me go did not make any sense to me. The company had a $300 bonus that they gave out every three months. I had a few creative ideas for ways to earn this bonus. I made a statement one day while at work that I wanted to make history. This was around the time of 9/11, and one of the workers went to the boss and repeated what I had said. I did not want to explain to the employee how I wanted to make history, because then I would have to explain my creative ideas. I did not want anybody stealing my ideas.

I went into work one day after that and did not even make it to my floor. A supervisor met me at the front door and asked me to follow her to her office. I did not expect to hear or receive what I got that day. As I followed her to her office, she rudely pointed her finger into my face and told me about what she had been informed. I was in shock, and I felt as if my stomach was going to hit the floor. She did not give me a chance to say one word or explain what I meant about making history. I was escorted from her office to the front door and immediately had to leave the property. She thought I was a terrorist. I felt horrible. I called the supervisor back on my way home and explained that if she would have given me a chance, she would have found out that I was speaking about getting the highest bonus of anyone in the company. I do not know how she felt when I told her this, but I was not asked to return to work.

I had a little bit of money saved up but signed up for unemployment until I found another job so that I could keep my home. I started scanning the paper and found a job to help flood victims that was contracting out of Charleston, West Virginia. I had an interview and was hired on the spot. This job was a grueling hourly job, and I did not know how long it would last. But it was my only source of income to consider at the time, so I took it. I had the opportunity of helping people find resources and give them comfort and support in their time of losing their homes due to the storms.

How ironic this was, To be helping people go through their storm when I was going through one too. It was not quite like mine, but I felt that God knew what he was doing and I was sure that there was something to be gained through this experience. I met some wonderful people, and my heart went out to each and every one of them. While there, Preston was back at the boot camp and doing what he was expected to do. He finished up the school year and passed again and was in Who's Who among American High School Students. I was very proud of him for this accomplishment. My new job was temporary, and I was unable to keep my home. I moved in with my boyfriend, Jay. This was a rocky time for both Jay and me. We were used to living by ourselves, but we tried to make the best out of a bad situation.

Chapter 12

The boot camp let Preston go because he was of age, and Preston called and asked me if he could move in with Jay and me. Jay and I discussed this, and Jay decided that Preston moving in was not a good idea. This caused some tension between us. Preston came home and stayed with my foster dad, Dave. Preston got a job at an amusement park for the summer working at a TGI Friday's restaurant. Preston had a few weeks to go before starting his job and would walk, or call me for a ride wherever he needed to go.

One evening Preston went to his friend Mike's home and called me for a ride to go back to my dad's home. I did not discuss with Jay where I was going, because Jay had a problem anytime I tried to do anything for my son. I did not want to argue, so I just told Jay that I had somewhere to go and asked him if he needed anything before I left. The phone rang before I reached the front door, but I did not stop to answer it. I left the house to pick Preston up and learned the phone call was from Preston. We arrived at my father's and I visited him a little bit. When I arrived back at Jay's home, I could see through the screen door that all my belongings were packed in garbage bags sitting on the kitchen floor, and I could not get into the house. The screen door was locked, preventing me from using my key. I called Jay, but he did not answer. I must have stayed out there for twenty minutes trying to get a response. I could not for the life of me understand why he was behaving this way. I ended up calling a girlfriend, and she put me up for the night.

The next morning I went back to Jay's to see if I could get some answers, but he didn't let me in. He had a sister who didn't live too far away, so I walked to her home. After telling her what had happened, she called Jay, and he answered the phone. She told him I wanted to see him. Finally, he opened the door when I returned, and the conversation was not good. He told me that he wanted me to leave because he thought I was seeing someone else. I told him that if he would have picked up the phone before I'd left, he would have found out that the other person was my son. He apologized and wanted me to stay, but I felt the damage had already been done. I did not want this to happen again, so I decided to leave. I arranged with my father that day to pick me up, and I moved out of Jay's home. Even though it felt horrible, I wondered if maybe it was a blessing in disguise.

I started a new life at my father's. Preston and I shared a small room together. My father lived in a trailer, which was small, but we made the best of it. I continued to look for employment. This transition of me leaving Jay was a lesson for me. I learned to put more trust in God and his timing for my life. I prayed more and waited for God to open another door for me. The job market was scarce around this time. I did not know what I would find, but I had God and my faith to rely on. God never let me down before, and I knew his love would prevail.

The day finally arrived for Preston to leave, and I thought this type of job would be wonderful for him. The amusement park would supply him with a room and food, and all he would be responsible for was washing his clothing and buying his hygiene products. He would even receive free rides when he was not working. This was going to be right up Preston's alley—the perfect job for him, I thought.

I was blessed to find a temporary job working at a bank as a loan processor for rates that were extremely low on homes during this time. I thanked God for opening this door for me and was grateful for the experience that I had working in the titles department in Pittsburgh. The management and their employees were exceptional to work for and gave me an income that I needed for a home. I continued to work and scour the ads in the paper.

The homes were selling fast, and I found no homes feasible for me to rent. I found an apartment, but it was not in the most decent neighborhood. This neighborhood used to be an upper-class neighborhood where you could raise your family with no problem. Time and crime had changed that, though. I really did not want to move there, but when I went to look at it, I changed my mind and found out; it was something I could afford. This apartment was well kept, and I did not have to bring a thing, as it was fully furnished. There were dishes, silverware, pots, and pans. It had two bedrooms, a nice-size living room, a spacious kitchen, a basement, and a washer and dryer. I had my own washer and dryer but just stored them in the basement. I could not get over how nice the inside of the apartment looked. It was too nice to be in this neighborhood. Everything appeared to be perfect for what I needed. I spoke with the person that was renting it and moved in.

Preston finished up the summer with the amusement park. He moved in with me, and I told him to look for work. I figured that as long as I went to work and minded my own business that everything would be peaceful. Preston met a boy named Marcus through Mike. Marcus happened to live across the street from us, and he and Preston became friends. Preston did not want to finish up the last year of high school. I did not want to fight this out with him, so I told him to at least get his GED.

Preston started his prep courses for his GED at our local collage, and in no time, he had the scores needed to pass. The college held a graduation ceremony for the graduates, and Preston wore a cap and gown. I was proud of him and thought it was nice to see him make such an accomplishment. Preston received a graduation ring from the college, and this made him happy. My older brother and I were the only ones in my family who graduated, and now to see Preston do this made me proud. He wanted to go to college up in Cincinnati, Ohio. I thought this was odd since he had not wanted to continue high school, but we discussed the importance of college and the responsibilities he would have if he were to go. Preston assured me that he would follow through on this and said that since he'd gotten his GED, he felt college was the right thing to do. As his mother, I wanted to give him every opportunity to succeed in life and was proud of him for making this decision.

I took one day off from my job to enroll him. He was accepted at Raymond Walters College and was going to major in veterinary technology. He loved animals, and I encouraged him in whatever he wanted to do. I wanted the best for him and knew that if he put his mind to it, he could do it. I took him shopping for his computer, bedding, refrigerator, microwave, writing paper, binders, and all the things he would need for his dorm. His friend Marcus was going to attend the same collage. Marcus was majoring in music.

I thought it was nice that the two of them would be attending the same college. Marcus and Preston would not be staying in the same dorm but would be in close proximity of each other. Preston and I spent a lot of time together before he left for college. I knew that I would not get to see him much and wanted to spend as much time with him as possible.

Chapter 13

The day finally arrived to move my son into his dorm. A lot of students were there that day carrying their suitcases and luggage. Preston and I unloaded the car and headed for the dorm. As we walked down the hall to his room, we peeked into the other rooms to see what they were like. There was just enough room for what he needed. There was a bed, a computer desk, a little kitchen area for his refrigerator, a closet, and a bathroom. I helped him make his bed and set his computer up. Preston put his dishes, food, towels, and clothes away and placed his microwave on his counter. He was excited that day. He hugged me and told me he loved me and to not worry and that he would keep in touch with me by phone. As I drove home that day my only hope was that Preston would be responsible and get himself up to go to his classes. I realized for the first time how grown up he was. He seemed to want this, and the thought of him going to college was wonderful.

Preston called me every evening, and everything seemed to be going well. He was going to his classes and handing in his homework on time. One evening he asked for $300 for some programs that he needed for his computer. I didn't think anything about it and sent him the money. I had no way to follow up with his teachers to find out if what he was saying was true, and I found out later that he had taken a bunch of his new friends out to eat and to party in a motel. I was not a millionaire and worked very hard for the money I made, and to think that it was going for something like this made me furious. When I spoke to him, I told him I did not appreciate his deception and that I would no longer send him money. I added that if he needed more, he would have to get a job and pay for the things that he needed. As the saying goes, "Fool me once, shame on you. Fool me twice, shame on me."

Preston continued with his schooling, and then about three months from the time he started, the school went on spring break. The next semester was going to be an expensive one. I thought for sure Preston would be covered on grants, but I was wrong. I set up an interview with the financial advisor by phone and found out that the next semester's tuition was not going to be covered by grants and wasn't something I could afford. Preston and I realized that he could not continue going.

He moved back home with me, and I told him to get a job. The job market in Steubenville, Ohio, was not good at the time, but I told him to just apply wherever he could. Preston asked me to buy him a car so that he could go look for work. I told him to find a job first and then we would see about him getting a car. He finally came to me one day and told me he'd found a job. "Let's go get a car," he said. I responded that he would need to work for a while first and then we would see about getting one.

Preston Found a job and was hired at a local Kroger store as a bagger. I don't think I have ever seen him so happy about a job in all my life. He came home one day and told me they were looking for someone to work in the meat department. I told him to speak to the manager if it was something he wanted to do and to learn everything there was to know in that department. The next day they moved him from bagger into the meat department. He absolutely loved this job. He came home smiling and appeared to look forward to going to work. I don't know what it was about this job that made him so happy, but I was pleased he had a job that he enjoyed and looked forward to going to. As the old saying goes, if you can find a job that you love, you will never have to work a day in your life. At age twenty, I think my son found that job. Preston worked only part-time, but he'd found something that made him happy, and I was happy for him. Things started to look up for him. When Preston was not working, he and his friend Mike would hang out together.

My temporary job at the bank ended. I loved this job and all the people I worked with. They left an everlasting impression on my heart. They had a party for me the day I left to let me know how much they all appreciated working with me. I cried and did not want to leave. I continued looking for employment and found a job bartending at a local bar. It was not something that I wanted to do, but I took it anyway. I paid myself out of the nightly till every night. The pay was not that great, but I kept hoping that maybe something better would come along.

I worked at the bar for three months and struck up a conversation with a regular customer. She worked at the local Conrail railroad station in Mingo Junction, Ohio, and told me I should apply. She brought me an application, and I filled it out and was hired. I quit the job bartending and started working for the railroad. This job was interesting. I would haul the railroaders to their destinations and get an hourly rate plus my mileage. I would work long hours before getting sleep, and this affected my eating patterns. I did love to travel, but this job reminded me of my biological father, who was a truck driver. I gained a newfound respect for truckers.

My son continued to work for Kroger, and things were going well. He met a girl through his friend Mike. Her name was Requena, and she and Preston started dating. We called her Ricky for short. After a while, wherever my son was, she was not far behind. She was a nice girl and made my son happy. Preston would be turning twenty-one in a few days, and Ricky and I went shopping for his birthday. Ricky bought him as much as I did, if not more. The day finally arrived for his party, and it was wonderful. A few of his closest friends attended. I stayed long enough for Preston to open all his presents and to enjoy a piece of his Steelers' football cake, and then I left for work. The birthday turned out to be one of the greatest birthdays of all. He had everything going for him. He had a girlfriend who cared for him and who was making a difference in his life, friends who supported and loved him, and a job. I could not believe that Preston was twenty-one and had a girlfriend. He'd grown up so fast.

One day Preston came to me and asked if Ricky could move in with us. He said her apartment was not getting fixed and was not a safe place to live. I told him that I did not see how that would work out for us. We were struggling as it was and did not have the room for her. I told him I did not approve of them sleeping in the same room together, which would create a problem. I could not imagine my son having sex in my home. I had many discussions with him on the subject of safe sex, but every time I brought up the subject, he would say, "I know, Mom." Preston assured me that none of that would be going on and that he would sleep on the couch and let her have his room. I could see where this was going and did not want to think about him sneaking into the bedroom, so I told him no. Preston was not happy with my decision but respected my answer and told me that he would never do anything to disrespect me. Preston had disrespected me in the past by going against my many wishes for him, and so I just told him that Ricky moving in was not going to happen.

Not long after this conversation, the upstairs apartment alongside mine became available. I told Preston that he and Ricky could apply for that one if they were interested. I thought it would be nice to have him close by me. He and Ricky did apply for the apartment and to my amazement moved in. I was a little afraid of this at first. Preston was only working part-time, and I did not know how he and Ricky were going to maintain the rent. Ricky did have a job, but I did not know her pay. I knew that Preston's job was not enough to sustain the rent. I told him that if ever he needed my help, I would help if I could. Preston was at my home every day asking what there was to eat. It was as though he had never moved out. I loved that about him. He was a hearty eater, and he could always count on Mom for a good meal.

Ricky and Preston visited me as much as they could. The day finally came for Preston to get a car. He wanted to go across the river to West Virginia to this used-car dealership. I gave him a set budget and told him not go over the amount that we discussed. The first car he brought home and showed me was clearly over our discussed budget. This was an example of him going against my wishes. I had to follow him back over to see what else they had that was feasible for our budget. I should have gone with him the first time, but I'd wanted to give him the benefit of the doubt to see if he could follow through with what we'd discussed. I was wrong.

The next car he saw was a beautiful candy-red Cadillac that was in our price range. There was nothing wrong with the car. It was clean and had low mileage, and I don't even think there was a scratch on it. I asked Preston what in the world he needed something so big for, and he said, "Mom, I am a big boy now, and I don't want to look like Fred Flintstone driving down the road in some small car." I just laughed. He loved that car, and his face lit up like a Christmas tree. His eyes were gleaming, and he kept rubbing the car with the sleeve of his shirt. I could not blame him. It was a pretty car. He took it for a test spin and came back and told me it ran like a gem. I explained to him that if there were any problems with this car, it wouldn't be cheap to fix it. I also had to remind him of his part-time job. He said, "It's okay, Mom; you will help me." I explained to him that if something big needed to be fixed, I would have to see what my pay was before fixing it. I had bills too. He assured me that he understood. He did not find anything else that day. He was sold on that Cadillac. I don't think I ever saw my son in as good of a mood as he was in that day. His whole life changed. I saw my son in a new light, and for the first time I actually thought, *Life is good.* He took pride in himself and appeared to appreciate what life had to offer him.

Not long after this he and Requena came to visit me, and my son said, "I am going to the store for a pickle."

I looked at Ricky as he walked out the door and asked if she was pregnant.

She just looked at me and asked, "Why?" I asked her if she had been craving pickles, and she said, "Yes, I have, but I'm not craving one right now."

I told her maybe the craving had passed to my son. I explained to her that I'd known couples in the past where the pregnant woman's partner would crave the same things she did.

They went the following day for a pregnancy test, and my instincts were correct. I was not happy about this and cried to Preston that he could not even take care of himself with a part-time job. How in the world was he going to take care of a baby? He reassured me that everything would be okay. I got in my car that day after hearing the news and just drove around crying and trying to come to some kind of acceptance.

I needed a break after hearing this news, and luckily, I had purchased a ticket with a meal to a Ronnie Milsap concert up in Pittsburgh at the Pepsi-Cola Roadhouse. On the night of the concert, I walked into the building and found my way over to the counters where they were selling items. I purchased a T-shirt and bought one of each of the CDs that they had on display. After buying the items, I found my seat. I was in the front row table, fourth seat. I had a perfect view of the stage, and the opportunity to see Ronnie Milsap like this was fantastic. I ate my meal and tried not to think of what had happened back home. I struck up a conversation with a woman across the table from me and told her about Ronnie being one of my favorite singers of all time. This concert was awesome, even better than I'd expected. Ronnie Milsap is an exceptional artist, and I was honored to see him perform in my lifetime.

Intermission came, and the same woman sitting across from me handed me a ticket and said, "Grab your coat and all your belongings, and follow me."

I looked at her and asked, "Why?"

She said, "Because you are going backstage to see Ronnie."

I looked at her in amazement with gleaming eyes and asked her if she was serious. She said yes. I was so happy that I started jumping up and down with joy. This was a once-in-a-lifetime opportunity, and for it to be given to me made me cry. I got up from my seat and hugged her and headed for the line that was forming. I could not believe this moment. Who was this woman that gave me this free pass? She told me she worked there and that it was her job to surprise people of her choosing. I was blessed that night and had a picture taken with him. I kissed him on his cheek and told him I loved him and had all his music. He turned and gave me a kiss and said, "Bless you, sweetheart." This was one night to remember, and it captured my heart like no other.

While driving home that night, I put in one of the CDs that I'd bought. I wasn't paying attention and missed my exit. I drove clear up to where I used to work and had to turn around and head back home. I was completely in awe of this night and smiled the whole way home. Ronnie's music always seemed to take me to another world. Preston came to visit me the next day and asked me how I enjoyed the concert. I told him it was an epic night to remember. We did not discuss anything about the pregnancy or how I felt about it.

This fact that Preston was going to be a father was going to take a few days to sink in. Everything appeared to be happening all at once. My baby had a part-time job, a girlfriend that appeared to make him happy, a baby on the way, and a car. Preston was on top of the world. He danced in the front yard screaming at the top of his lungs that he was going to be the daddy that he never knew. I did not want to put a damper his spirits, but I was not feeling this joy at all.

About a week after the Ronnie Millsap concert, I came to the realization that things were not going to change and accepted reality for what it was. I had a meeting of the minds with myself so to speak. I sat down and wrote a long letter to Preston. I told him what a joy he had been in my life and said that if this made him happy, I would support him in any way that I could. I spoke of all the fun times we had and of our hardships. I told him that I would not change anything for the world. I spoke of the love I had for him and wanted him to know how much he meant to me and how I wanted the best for him. I wrote about all the growing-up years and how the painful times helped in making him who he was. I said that our lives never turn out exactly how we plan them to be but that we should learn to accept them and do what we can to embrace the change.

Little did I realize that this letter would be the last meaningful conversation I would have with Preston. Nothing in the world could have prepared me for what I had to face in the days ahead.

Chapter 14

The morning of March 17, 2006, was no different from any other morning except for Preston coming to tell me he was not feeling well. He told me his sinuses were bothering him and that he could not breathe. I had some Tylenol on hand and suggested he take that. He looked in the refrigerator, got a bite to eat, and said he was going home to lie down. Preston didn't have to work this day and was waiting for Ricky to return from work. It was Preston's payday, and he and Ricky always tried to go somewhere and do something together on payday.

The man I was dating at the time had just gotten off from work and called to ask if I wanted to get some lunch. He picked me up, and we headed over across the river to a place that served the best fish in town. We were not gone long at all. We ate our fish and then left and drove straight back to my apartment. I was not in my apartment more than ten minutes when my phone rang. It was Preston's ex-girlfriend calling to ask me if he was okay. I didn't know what she meant. I told her he was okay and hung up the phone. The phone rang again, and this time it was Preston's ex-girlfriend's sister on the other end crying and saying she hoped Preston was not dead. I told her he was fine and hung up the phone. I don't know why I didn't ask her what she was talking about, since this was strange. I no sooner hung up the phone than it rang again. This time the brother of the two girls had called to ask if I was sure Preston was okay. I said yes, that he was upstairs sleeping. The brother asked me again if I was sure. I looked out my front window, and Preston's car was not parked out front.

My heart started to sink. I knew something was wrong. I fell to my knees and started to cry. I did not know what was wrong but knew I needed to call the hospital or police, though I didn't know whom to call first. I chose the hospital, and the attending nurse that answered the phone put me on hold for what seemed like an eternity. She finally returned and said an officer would be at my house to speak to me. I did not know what to think. The anticipation of not knowing what was going on was killing me inside. I waited for what seemed a lifetime. The officer finally arrived and told me the news of my son's passing. The officer did not have all the details yet, but he told me that my son had passed away and that they were going to investigate the matter. Ricky was off of work and sitting at my kitchen table when the officer arrived. We asked all kinds of questions that the officer clearly could not answer. We both were numb and could not believe this type of thing could have happened to someone as wonderful as my Preston.

We left my home that afternoon and headed to the hospital. The room they had him in was the last room in the emergency room. I ran to the doorway and could not push the curtains back fast enough to find my son lying there. I wanted answers and fast. The officer had not told me he had been shot. I wasn't told this until arriving at the hospital. He just looked as if he was sleeping. I ran over to him, and his body was still warm. I cried for him to wake up, but his eyes would not open. "Why is my baby sleeping and not waking up?" I cried. I could not for the life of me figure this out. I was in shock, and a man was standing at the foot of my son's bed. *Why is he here? Who is he? I will just wake my son up, and we will leave. This is not real. It is just a dream.*

The more I tried to make sense of everything, the more confusing it was. A nurse came in to ask me what funeral home I wanted to go with. I just looked at her as if she were crazy. My son was an eye donor, and the people at the hospital wanted me to speak to someone on the phone about this. Things were happening too fast, and I could not think straight or get it out of my head that my son was dead. I just wanted him to wake up and come home with me. The officers arrived at the hospital and wanted to question me on who I thought could have done this and why. I was oblivious to what was going on. I just wanted to die. Was my son dead? Or was I in a bad dream?

My sister-in-law was at the emergency room for some reason that day. I hollered at her in the parking lot to tell her the news. She yelled at me, and I didn't know why and didn't ask. I told her Preston had passed away, and she called my brother, who came out to be with me. The officers asked me something, and my brother said something outlandish to them, and I got upset. This whole ordeal was a mess, and I could not understand any of it. My son never hurt a soul and was well liked by many. Why in the world would anyone take his life? This was a mystery to me. This was the worst day of my life, and I kept telling myself it was a dream and that Preston was going to wake up any minute. I wanted to hold him, and that is what I did. He looked so peaceful lying there, and all I could do was talk to him, but he did not respond. I was heartbroken. My baby had never slept this long. *Wake up, Preston! Wake up!* The attending nurse that was dealing with my son came in to tell me that they had to take him. I clung onto him for dear life. I just wanted to stay with him and never let him go.

I aged twenty or thirty years that day. My baby was gone, and how in the world was I going to go on without him? That night was the longest night of my life. I did not want to go to sleep, because I thought Preston was going to come through the front door. He always played pranks on me, and I wanted to believe that this one was one of them. I finally fell asleep from pure exhaustion and woke up to a voice in my ear that said, "Prepare for battle." I did not know what to make of that voice. It was a though someone was standing over me and said this. I know this voice was as real as I am alive today. I woke up and went to the living room, and Ricky was sleeping on the couch. I cried out, "What does that mean?" I was never so scared in all my life. I desperately needed to find the answer to the voice. The officers had to do their investigation, and I did not know how long it would be before I found out exactly what had happened.

I went to the store that morning and bought a pack of cigarettes. I looked at all the people in the store as though they were the ones to blame. There were people in the store who questioned why this happened and offered their condolences to me. One person said it happened because they wanted his car. I had just bought that car for him ten days ago. I felt horrible and thought it was my fault. I left there in a hurry and scurried home as fast as I could. I still did not want to believe this. I got home and sat at the table and started going through all of Preston's pictures and then went to sit at the computer I'd bought for him.

Preston's screen saver read, "Preston Loves Requena." While I was sitting there, the screen saver started jumping all over the screen. Ricky was sitting at the table, and I told her to look at the screen. The more I told her about what the screen saver was doing, the faster it moved. We both could not believe what we were seeing. I told her that Preston was here with us. We were in awe of it and could not take our eyes off of the screen. I so did not want to believe this. I was still hoping to see him walk through the front door. We listened for his voice to come through the computer, but all we got was the fast movement from the screen saver. Ricky and I both knew that this was Preston's spirit. I was not touching the screen, and we both just kept watching and hoping for more of what Preston would do. As tears ran down my face, I kept telling myself this wasn't happening. I was totally numb and in a fog and tried so desperately to figure this entire thing out.

The phone kept ringing, and people kept knocking at my door. I wanted this day to go away. The TV news had broadcast about Preston being shot in his car. I knew at this point that this was not a dream or a prank. I was so lost and did not know what to do. How in the world was I going to bury the one person who meant the world to me? I cried so hard and screamed at the TV. I visualized in my mind back to when he was little up until now. All I wanted were those years back. All I had now were my memories and pictures to remind me of what once was. I thought of Ricky and my grandbaby being without his father. I lost all hope and my will to survive. Preston so desperately wanted to be the father that he never knew, and now that was taken away from him. My grandbaby was going to be fatherless. This was something that Ricky and I both would have to face. We both tried so hard to deal with this fate as the days progressed. It was like a dream that had gone bad.

The morning before Preston passed, instead of lying down to rest, he had taken a shower. I learned that he had gone to his job, picked up his check, filled his car with gas, and then gone to the car wash. Preston had then gone to a store that was four blocks from our home. Two boys were standing in front of the store. One boy Preston knew, and the other he did not know. Preston proceeded into the store and bought a Black and Mild cigarette and a Mountain Dew. He came across another boy that he knew. This boy approached Preston and asked for a ride off the hill. As Preston walked out of the store, the boy that was in the store followed him, along with the other two that were outside. Preston gave the boys a ride off the hill that morning and headed to downtown Steubenville. One of the boys stuck a gun to my son's head while Preston was driving and demanded his money. My son sped up and turned on a side street and ran into a telephone pole. I knew that my son had been trying to scare them and distract them from shooting him in the head. Preston had been shot in the back when this happened, and the three boys had fled the scene. It took three days for the boys to be caught, and they all were sentenced.

It took nine days after Preston's passing for me to go to the funeral home to pick out his casket. The funeral director had a problem with accepting funds that a friend wanted to provide. The prosecutor's office secretary had arranged for the Victims Assistance Fund to cover the cost. This was the hardest day in my life. Who would have thought that something like this could happen to their child? I just was not prepared. I could not do it alone, so I called my foster dad, Dave, to accompany me on this journey. Dave had lost his wife, Preston's grandmother, in 2002, so this was hard for him. He still agreed to accompany me. I cried the whole time and didn't understand anything about this process at all. The funeral director took me to all the caskets and showed me what they had to offer. I picked out the nicest one that they could provide for me and some other things that would be needed for the services. I had never in all my life understood what it was like to bury someone, but I found out that day. My father, Dave, did the nicest thing for Preston that day and gave up his graveyard plot, which helped tremendously in costs. It was a gesture of love on his part, and I will be indebted to him forever. Preston was very close to his grandma and grandpa, and I am sure this would please him.

Two days after picking out the casket, the day of the services arrived, and I could not stand to greet all the people that came in that day. I sat up in front, and all the people came to where I was sitting to offer their condolences. I was totally lost within myself and could not even remember who some of the people were, even though I had known them for a while. This was a nightmare that I was going to have to live with forever. After the services were over, Ricky and I went up to the casket to say our good-byes. We both kissed and hugged him tightly. Ricky was five months' pregnant, and I hoped that the remaining days would be all right for her.

We left the funeral home and headed for the burial site. Preston was placed next to his grandma, and all of us gathered around the casket and waited for the service to start to say our final good-byes. Preston's and my life together as we knew it was over that day, and it broke my heart so much. Preston was my world, and I did not want to part with him. The reality of this made me tremble. As we started to leave, my dad nudged me on the arm and told me that he had seen my foster mom and Preston holding hands next to a tree that was in the corner. I knew at that moment that my son was in good hands. As the tears rolled down my face, I felt some relief to know that my mom was with him and would be seeing him through to the next journey of his life. My son had his whole world ahead of him in this life, but God called him home to be by his side. My son's dream of being the father he never knew or becoming a veterinary technician did not come to pass, but through this memoir, his dream can flourish and last. Preston will always be remembered for the kind and loving spirit that he was and for the zest he had for life.

Grandma Janice and Preston.

Made in the USA
Coppell, TX
21 May 2020